W9-CGT-613

12/28/01

Global Trends and Global Governance

Edited by
Paul Kennedy, Dirk Messner and Franz Nuscheler

Pluto Press
LONDON • STERLING, VIRGINIA

and

Development and Peace Foundation

First published 2002 by Pluto Press
345 Archway Road, London N6 5AA
and 22883 Quicksilver Drive,
Sterling, VA 20166–2012, USA

www.plutobooks.com

British Library Cataloguing in Publication Data
A catalogue record for this book is available from the British Library

Library of Congress Cataloging in Publication Data
Global trends and global governance / edited by Paul Kennedy, Dirk
Messner and Franz Nuscheler.
     p. cm.
   ISBN 0–7453–1751–0 (hardback) — ISBN 0–7453–1750–2 (paperback)
   1. Globalization. 2. International organization. I. Kennedy, Paul M.,
   1945– II. Messner, Dirk. III. Nuscheler, Franz.
   JZ1318 .G564 2001
   327—dc21
                                                                    2001002158

ISBN 0 7453 1751 0 hardback
ISBN 0 7453 1750 2 paperback

11   10   09   08   07   06   05   04   03   02
10   9   8   7   6   5   4   3   2   1

Designed and produced for Pluto Press by
Chase Publishing Services, Fortescue, Sidmouth EX10 9QG
Typeset from disk by Stanford DTP Services, Towcester
Printed in the European Union by The Cromwell Press, Trowbridge, England

Contents

Preface   vii

**1 Global Challenges at the Beginning of the
   Twenty-First Century**   1
   Paul Kennedy
   Demographic Trends   2
   The Gap between Rich and Poor Societies   7
   The Technological Explosion: Prometheus Unbound   10
   Environmental Pressures   12
   Security Problems: More Weapons of Mass Destruction   13
   Transborder Diseases   15
   Global Trends: Confusion and Contradiction   16
   Conclusion: Should We be Optimistic or Pessimistic?   19

2 World Society – Structures and Trends   22
   Dirk Messner
   World Society: Reality or Phantom?   23
   The Great Challenge of the Twenty-First Century:
   Civilizing the Global Market Economy   34
   Building Structures Keyed to World Society   40
   Future Prospects and Challenges   58

3 World Economy – Structures and Trends   65
   Heribert Dieter
   The World Economy at the Outset of the Twenty-First
   Century   67
   Regionalism   77
   Measures Aimed at Stabilizing the World Economy   82

4 World Ecology – Structure and Trends   97
   Udo Ernst Simonis and Tanja Brühl
   Causes of Environmental Degradation   98
   The Need for Action: Strengthening Global
   Environmental Governance   102

Global Environmental Governance: Aims, Instruments,
and Institutions   107
Innovations in Global Environmental Governance   115
Future Political Options   121

5   **World Politics – Structures and Trends**   125
    Dirk Messner and Franz Nuscheler
    New Turbulences and Anarchic Tendencies   126
    Shifting Conceptions of the World: A Multipolar or
    a Unipolar World Order?   133
    New Structural Elements of World Politics in the
    'Age of Globalism'   141
    Perspectives and Options: Superpower Governance
    versus Global Governance?   149

6   **Global Governance, Development, and Peace**   156
    Franz Nuscheler
    Globalization: Is the World Still Governable?   156
    Building Blocks of a Global Governance Architecture   159
    Presuppositions of Global Governance   162
    Contradictions between Insights and Action   164
    Global Governance, Development, and Peace   168
    Perspectives of the Global Government Project:
    Vision or Illusion?   181

7   **Globalization and Global Governance – A Synopsis**   184

Notes on the Contributors   196
Index   198

Preface

This book presents five contributions published under the title *Global Trends 2000* by the German Development and Peace Foundation, which was founded by Willy Brandt. A sixth contribution deals with the publication of the *Brandt Report* some 20 years ago. What answers would the group of prominent political figures (which included Edward Heath, Shridath Ramphal, and Edgard Pisani) then assembled around Willy Brandt come up with today to the challenges facing humanity at the beginning of the twenty-first century? In his introductory essay, Paul Kennedy provides an outline of these challenges, which, without exaggeration, one can call dramatic.

Global Trends and Global Governance presents analyses of important developments in world society, the world economy, world ecology, and world politics. The contributors have set themselves the task of illustrating how global problems are linked, which is referred to in the current discussion, perhaps somewhat fuzzily, as globalization, and coming up with some prophetic answers to the question of the direction in which the world is heading at the beginning of the twenty-first century.

The six contributors not only analyze some of the central development trends in a complex world, they also seek to elucidate what, at different levels of action, politics could and should do to devise solutions to pressing world problems. Is the world still governable, and if so, how? Some answers are offered by the concept of global governance, elaborated in 1995 by the International Commission on Global Governance in its report *Our Global Neighbourhood* and further developed by the German Development and Peace Foundation in cooperation with the Institute for Development and Peace of the University of Duisburg.

The six contributions to this volume combine scholarly analysis with recommendations for political action. In view of the fact that behind the scenes of government actors from civil society are increasingly actively involved in shaping the process of globalization, these recommendations are addressed not only to governments but also to individuals and social groups. The aim of global governance is more multilateralism in order come to terms cooperatively with problems of a transnational nature. At the same time, it sets its sights on a new model of politics that might be characterized as a public/private partnership.

Paul Kennedy, Dirk Messner, Franz Nuscheler

1
Global Challenges at the Beginning of the Twenty-First Century

Paul Kennedy

The greatest difficulty we have in describing our global condition as we enter the twenty-first century is that the picture that presents itself is so mixed. Measured in terms of personal prosperity, about one-sixth of the world's population now enjoys an uncommonly high standard of living, This includes a much smaller percentage who have achieved extraordinary levels of wealth. Another third of humanity, in the so-called emerging economies, have seen rapid increases in per capita income over the past quarter-century; yet about one-half of the inhabitants of the globe are still battling against often extreme poverty. The same polarization can be found in the realms of justice, human rights, democracy, war, and peace. States in, say, Scandinavia enjoy a happy combination of high prosperity, environmental care, social services, and political and all other freedoms, whereas many countries in, say, Africa lag far behind on almost all counts.

Such an extraordinarily mixed picture may be beyond our comprehension and too often leads observers to describe only partial accounts of the untidy, larger whole. Thus, the 'cornucopian' school paints an exciting scene of a high-tech nirvana which all may enjoy, whilst doom-mongers warn that we are crossing environmental and demographic thresholds that can only lead to disaster (cf. Kennedy 1993). The challenge in producing such a work as *Global Trends and Global Governance* is to capture the varieties of this mixed landscape, yet at the same time avoid blandness and a lack of commitment.

Perhaps the best way to think about where our planet is heading is to attempt to produce what Nobel scientist Murray Gell-Mann often refers to as 'a crude look at the whole.' One suspects that such a description might best be done by a social anthropologist or a geographer, or at the very least by a scholar-observer who is willing to describe the totality of our human activities and the contexts in which they take place. Instead of the world of, say, the Trobriand Islanders being the subject of study, it would be the world of – well – our entire earth. Its approach would be 'ecological' in the largest sense of that word. What follows is one person's modest attempt in that direction.

The first and most basic fact of existence is that, unless we manage to blow up humanity and everything else in the decades to come, this is a *live* planet unlike the others in the galaxy. Not only does the earth breathe and change with the seasons and the daily ritual of rainfall and evaporation, but it contains millions of species which are also living, breathing, and active. Of all those species – birds, animals, fish, insects, reptiles – one in particular is dominant: *Homo sapiens*, a two-legged mammal of various colors and sizes and two genders, which lives about 75 years on average, and dwells on land rather than in the water or the air. This species has other notable characteristics. It forms societies of many sorts and numbers, it is immensely creative, it dominates all other species, it has increasing control of the natural environment, and, for better or worse, it has immense powers of destruction, both locally or globally. No other species does what it does: reading, inventing, dropping bombs, watching television, creating a United Nations, making money. No other species is interested in 'global trends,' or would even comprehend the term.

Demographic trends

So the real focus of any 'ecological' analysis of the future of our planet must be upon humankind itself, what *it* is up to, and where *it* is going. That being the case, it is best to start with some raw statistics about *Homo sapiens*. As we entered the twenty-first century, the number of human beings surpassed six billion. Yet just a half-century ago, within the lifetime of many alive today, the figure was some 2.5 billion. This is an absolute increase that far exceeds that which has occurred in any other period of human experience. It took until 1825 to reach one billion humans *in toto*; it took only the next 100 years to double; and the next 50 years to double again, to 4 billion in 1975. A quarter of a century later, as we were celebrating the millennium, the total jumped to six billion. True, the pace of increase has been slowing in the last decade or so but, like a large oil tanker decelerating at sea, that slowdown is a protracted process.

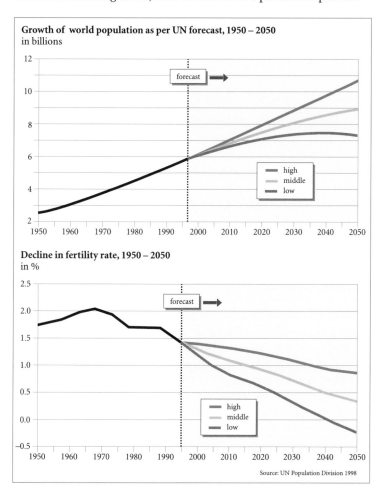

Figure 1.1

How long this will continue, and at what rate, is a topic that demographers, healthcare planners, economists, non-governmental organizations (NGOs), and international agencies are earnestly debating, and for good reason. Population change is affected by all sorts of variables, and projections that seemed feasible a decade ago for a country's total size by (say) the year 2020 can swiftly become out of date. We may be in for great surprises yet. Still, we know how many young women and girls of future child-bearing age are alive today, and on current evidence it is not unreasonable to assume that the earth may be host to about eight billion humans in 2025 and perhaps nine billion in 2050.

To repeat, whilst the relative pace of increase is clearly slowing, the rise in absolute numbers of human beings requiring sustenance, healthcare, jobs, housing, education, and a safe environment is daunting. So, too, could be the political and military implications of these demographic pressures. If six billion people can produce so much conflict over various causes, from territory to ideology, will a world of nine billion do any better?

Regional differences in demographic trends

We will return to these issues later in this chapter. But the teasing out of the demographic trends calls for more immediate attention. If the addition of some three billion people to the human total in the next half-century were spread evenly across the inhabitable parts of the globe, the challenges would be formidable, though under certain circumstances it probably could be managed. But the fact is that these increases will not be uniform across the regions. There is, as we know, a massive difference in demographic trends occurring between rich countries and poor countries.

It is a commonplace to say that, roughly speaking, the peoples of the earth are divided into two types: those in what are called developed regions which are rich, technological societies, and those living in developing countries, which are usually much poorer and suffer considerable social and economic hardships. The really interesting thing is that the total population of the richer lands is expected to increase hardly at all over the next 50 years, whereas in the developing regions population growth is very rapid indeed. One might have thought that the richer population, enjoying an abundance of resources, would want to have large families, and that the poorer would fear having a large family. Humans, however, don't think like that.

Generally, the rich spend their money on material goods rather than on more children; while the poorest societies have the greatest tendency to produce large families even if it strains local resources and threatens their environment. When this discrepancy is broken down by region into forecasts of population increases, the pattern is confirmed: Africa, Asia, and Latin America expect big rises in overall population; North America will experience modest increases (chiefly through immigration); and Europe and Japan will probably decline in absolute numbers.

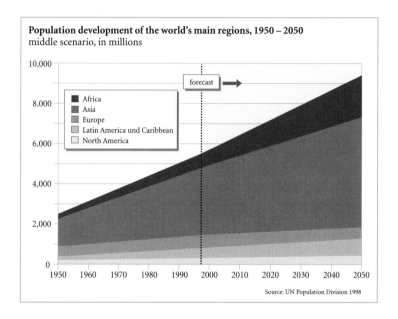

Population development of the world's main regions, 1950 – 2050
middle scenario, in millions

Legend:
- Africa
- Asia
- Europe
- Latin America und Caribbean
- North America

forecast

Source: UN Population Division 1998

Figure 1.2

Unless there are dramatic (and most unusual) changes in fertility rates in both developed and developing societies, the planet will have many more Indians and Iranians in a half-century's time, and significantly fewer Italians, Germans, and Japanese.

Two observations are worth making about this very skewed pattern of population change. One is obvious, but acutely sensitive politically – so much so that when the author raised it at a conference on population issues about a decade ago, he was publicly attacked by a member of the audience for having the nerve even to mention it. It is that this is not merely a matter of demographics; it is also one of geopolitics.

An historical anecdote captures the point best. We now know from recently released US records that, a full half-century ago, President Eisenhower was telling his closest advisors that he feared the long-term consequences of a population shift between 'the West and the Rest' – feared, that is, that the shift was away from the West (cf. Connelly and Kennedy 1994). At that time, about 28 per cent of the population lived in the industrialized democracies; but by the mid-point of the year 2000, only 12–13 per cent did; and it is estimated that, by the year 2050, the figure may be as low as about 8 per cent. One gets the impression that Eisenhower had a greater long-term fear of the 'population bomb' – to borrow the title of Ehrlich's famous book – than of nuclear bombs.

Mass migration from South to North?

The actual percentage shifts in the 'North/South' demographic balance matter less than the fact that they are real and substantial, and that they form the background to continuing political sensitivity about race, color, culture, and the gaps between rich and poor. To a Martian or any other extra-terrestrial observer, we earthlings look much the same everywhere, so the issue is unimportant. But to many politicians and citizens in the richer countries, it leads to alarm about being 'swamped' by poor immigrants, fears of a relative loss of influence in world affairs, and concern that the West's culture will be marginalized through sheer force of numbers.

What makes this intriguing is that the socio-economic and technological 'gap' between rich and poor societies is not accompanied by complete and insurmountable geographical and physical barriers. It is true that Africa is separated from prosperous Europe by the Mediterranean, and the Rio Grande separates the rich United States from its poorer neighbors to the South. But those boundaries are porous – especially the latter – and the US is actively leading a campaign for the ever-increasing integration of all societies, aided by technologies such as the Internet and the television, increased travel opportunities, student exchanges, massive investments of private capital in overseas countries, and by cultural interactions and international organizations. It is hard to imagine that all of what the classical economists termed the 'factors of production' can be globalized and liberalized without labor itself also becoming more mobile. Yet how many people in the richer countries are willing to admit large flows of people from the South, seeking employment in the North?

It also leads, interestingly, to gender tensions in richer societies, with some (generally conservative, and usually male) advocating increases in the national fertility rate, while other (generally liberal, and usually female) voices object to such natalist pressures and the motives behind them. Sensing these fears, spokesmen and women and intellectuals in developing countries argue that a wealthy minority are seeking to hang on to their disproportionate share of wealth and other advantages, and that the transfer of funds to assist population control in poorer countries is motivated by selfishness rather than altruism. For reasons to be explored later, it is difficult to persuade them otherwise.

The 'population supertanker' might slow down

The second consideration suggests an altogether more optimistic scenario. It is, after all, not inevitable that there will be nine billion people on the planet by 2050. That is the best rough projection we have at the moment, but our 'population supertanker' might slow down faster than we anticipate. In Brazil, for example, the fertility rate halved within about one generation, and dramatic surprises have occurred in the rates of population increase in such states as Egypt, Kenya, and Bangladesh, which a few years ago were regarded as much less likely to achieve reductions.

Regardless of what the West thinks or fears, a demographic transition would be good for developing countries *for their own sakes*. Thus, while Indian intellectuals, say, may suspect the richer countries of hypocrisy in promoting population control, it will not be a blessing for India to surge to a total population of 1.4–1.6 billion in a few decades' time; a smaller increase would ease the pressure on educational and social services, ease strains in the environment, and arguably lead to higher per capita incomes. Were more and more countries to achieve a democratic transition during the next few years, then all sides would be better off. The point is that no single voice in the current population debate can direct the future; but around three billion individual men and women, that is, today's and tomorrow's parents, certainly do.

The gap between rich and poor societies

The second important global trend which a social anthropologist would have to consider is the wealth-creating capacities of human beings, which once again distinguishes them from all other species on the earth. This is not an appropriate place for a survey of world history to discuss the impacts of the invention of the wheel, the sailing ship, or the steam engine, banking, or the spread of commerce, each of which has contributed to the growth of overall world product. But a quick reflection on the past century alone points to some important lessons – and to a probable (though again, not inevitable) future.

In the half-century up to 1950, humans experienced a rapid expansion of trade and industry, but then went into a catastrophic world war, a half-hearted recovery, a dreadful economic depression, and a second major conflict that laid low many of the industrial economies in the North. Learning the lesson from all this, and terrified by the power of the weapons of mass destruction they had invented, human society has managed to avoid any further all-out war between the Great Powers, and concentrated chiefly on economic growth, in line with the rising expectations of the postwar generations. Of course, there were fluctuations, but the overall trend was clear: gross world product doubled, and re-doubled, and doubled again between 1950 and 2000.

So how might things look for our planet if such an overall rate of growth continued – again with temporal and regional fluctuations – well into the present century? Some predictions assume an average annual increase of 3 per cent, some are much higher than this, yet others are more cautious. All economists and statisticians know the pitfalls of projecting trends in this linear fashion.

Yet, as with the population projections, once one begins to dis- aggregate the overall economic growth and income figures, either on a regional or a rich country/poor country basis, massive differ- ences in the standards of living of the earth's inhabitants emerge – indeed, they stand out. A half-century ago, the gap in living standards between the US and Canada on the one hand, and China and central Africa on the other, say, was enormous. Yet, despite the vast increase in world output since then, and the economic successes of many countries in Asia and Latin America, the gap between the really rich and the really poor is perhaps even more severe today.

This would be intriguing to an extra-terrestrial observer. Yet, it rarely occurs to us to think that all the earth's other species – be it sheep, cod, or sparrows – have roughly the same standards of living and consume roughly the same amounts as every other sheep, cod, or sparrow each day. But human beings have permitted a situation to arise in which certain of their societies enjoy levels of consumption 200 times greater than other societies.

Table 1.1   Gap between rich and poor regions and selected countries

(GDP per capita, PPP US$ 1998)*

Country	Income	Country	Income
US	29,605	Russian Federation	6,460
Kuwait	25,314	Thailand	5,456
Singapore	24,210	China	3,105
Canada	23,582	Indonesia	2,651
Japan	23,257	India	2,077
UK	20,336	Pakistan	1,715
Korea, Republic	13,478	Haiti	13,83
Chile	8,787	Nigeria	795
Brazil	6,625	Tanzania	480

Region/Group		Region/Group	
OECD	20,357	South-East Asia/Pacific	3,234
Latin America and Caribbean	6,510	South Asia	2,112
Eastern Europe/CIS	6,200	Sub-Saharan Africa	1,607
Arab States	4,140	LDC**	3,270
East Asia (excluding China)	13,635	LLDC***	1,064

*PPP=Purchasing Power Parity; ** LDC=Less Developed Countries;
*** Least Developed Countries
Source: Human Development Report 2000.

What is more, some forecasters, notably Hammond (1998), argue that this 'snapshot' of global disparities will change little between 2000 and 2050. As his projection shows, standards of living are expected to rise everywhere; but they will rise considerably faster in some parts of the world than in others, and from a higher take-off point, so that the relative gap between rich and poor might well remain much the same at the end of this period as it was at the beginning. Of course, a 50-year projection is a bold thing to attempt, and it is unlikely to be completely accurate. Yet even if it comes fairly close to the mark, and the population projections discussed earlier also turn out to be more or less accurate, then the social and political history of the twenty-first century may not be a very happy one.

The technological explosion: Prometheus unbound

But demographic changes and economic growth, both acting in uneven fashion and in many ways *inter*acting with each other, are not the only broad forces transforming our planet as the twenty-first century unfolds. Equal attention has to be given, surely, to the sheer explosion of science and technology in recent decades. It is true that human ingenuity has been making its mark for millennia, and also true that ever since the Industrial Revolution the interaction of science, technology, and economics – releasing humankind's energies just like Prometheus unbound (Landes 1976) – has accelerated that upward spiral in a seemingly unstoppable way. However, it is hard to believe that the flurry of inventions of the past 50 or so years – jet aircraft, telecommunications, great advances in biotechnology and health sciences, space exploration, to name but a few – is not transforming our lives in an even more intense and rapid way than in any previous era.

Figure 1.3

It is not easy to represent graphically the overall advance in science and technology, but the burgeoning of patent applications in recent times captures a little of this ferment. What is the most impressive aspect here is the incredible acceleration of pace.

This factor is important for at least two reasons. First, these scientific and technological advances were chiefly responsible for the overall growth of world product and wealth. The increases in prosperity in the 1950s were directly connected to the expansion in car ownership and air travel. Expansion in the 1990s was equally clearly boosted by the more efficient use of computers to increase output. It is easy to imagine a surge in the 2020s being much influenced by the first practical applications of the DNA revolution, which were only theoretical two decades ago. Nor is any of this surprising. Even as early as 1990, it was estimated that 85 per cent of all the scientists and technologists who had ever existed were alive at that moment. No wonder there was a technological explosion! Moreover, and in response to the sense that there are no limits to technology-driven growth, countries, companies, and universities everywhere, from Sweden to Brazil, have been pouring more and more resources into scientific research, so that the upward spiral continues.

Still, this too is unbalanced, as can be seen in Table 1.2, which shows the current use of the Internet. Perhaps 30 per cent of Americans now use the Internet daily; but only 0.1 per cent of sub-Saharan Africans do. Social and educational planners in richer countries are increasingly wringing their hands at the so-called 'digital gap' within their communities; but, while serious, that hardly compares to the 300:1 'gap' between American and African usage of the Internet. Yet without electricity and other infrastructure improvements, combined with a phenomenal rise in educational levels, how can Africa ever catch up?

It cannot be denied that the scientific and technological advances over the past 50 years have been beneficial to the human race overall. So, too, has been the sustained economic growth, even though that trend, like the pattern of population growth over the twentieth century, has revealed disturbing differences in the enjoyment of such benefits. Without doubt, many more people were enjoying a better standard of living in 2000 than was the case in 1950. And it is not unreasonable to forecast that these developments will continue, so that even more of the earth's inhabitants will enjoy better living standards by 2050 and 2100, even if many still lag behind.

Table 1.2   Internet users – a global enclave (1998)

Region/Country	Regional population as per cent of world population	Internet users as per cent of regional population
OECD (excl. US)	14.1	6.9
USA	4.7	26.3
Latin America/Caribbean	6.8	0.8
East Asia	22.2	0.4
South-East Asia/Pacific	8.6	0.5
South Asia	23.5	0.04
Arab States	4.5	0.2
Eastern Europe/CIS	5.8	0.4
Sub-Saharan Africa	9.7	0.1

Source: Human Development Report 1999: 63.

An overall rosy future, then? Perhaps, but there are at least three other global trends that would probably be noted in any broad look at the whole which might give cause for pause during this assessment of the world's prospects.

Environmental pressures

The first is the very serious indications of environmental pressures building up, quite naturally, as the consequence of two developments: the increases in the world's population and the even greater increases in economic activity and its impact on our natural surroundings. Forests are being cleared at a record pace, oceans are being over-fished, water supplies are diminishing in the critical regions of the Near East and northern India, and, above all, world temperatures, and in some regions especially, are rising too fast for comfort. The expected rise in sea levels, for example, is particularly significant, since that would affect the majority of inhabitants of the globe who, for various and obvious reasons, live close to the seashore and river banks.

On the other hand, it is also likely that, over the next few decades, a significant number of middle-income countries will wake up to the folly of environmental degradation and take steps to protect their forests, clean up their rivers, and reduce emissions – just as the

Europeans and Americans did 100 years ago following their own 'dirty' industrialization, and richer Asian states like Singapore are doing today, as their own wealthy middle classes demand, and pay for, a cleaner environment. Nevertheless, environmental improvement is generally specific and local and does not usually stray beyond the vicinity of the immediate actors. Ecologically-concerned residents of the village of Biggleswick are not especially worried about the fate of distant Smuggleswick, unless its damage has spillover effects.

Protecting the global commons is much harder to achieve politically, and it seems probable that neither North nor South, rich nor poor, will be willing to take all the steps necessary, to make all the sacrifices required, to reduce or even stabilize the overall trace gas emissions, short of some environmental disaster that sounds the tocsin for change. We can therefore expect average temperatures later in the twenty-first century to be between 4 and 8 °C higher, with knock-on consequences for the tempo of the growing seasons, coastal flooding, energy demand, water supply, and freak weather conditions of an ever more furious nature. Furthermore, the linkages between environmental instability on the one hand, and social and political instability on the other, though trickier to prove scientifically than to suspect instinctively, may well be much more evident.

Security problems: more weapons of mass destruction

Second is a very different sort of danger to the future of humankind, namely the increase in the number of states and other actors possessing weapons of mass destruction. In 1950, two countries had atomic weapons, although the US and USSR were soon joined by China, Britain, and France. This nuclear pentarchy – perhaps not coincidentally the five permanent members of the UN Security Council – managed to restrain themselves from unleashing their weapons for more than a half-century after Hiroshima, and gradually developed a mutual sense of 'living with the bomb' – but never using it.

At the beginning of the present century, however, this cozy pentarchical system is breaking down. More countries – Israel, India, and Pakistan are the most obvious – have become open or clandestine nuclear powers. Others, such as Brazil and Japan, have the capacity to become a nuclear power. 'Rogue' states, such as Libya, Iraq, and North Korea, are striving to join the club. Clearly, creating a nuclear war-fighting capacity is not a simple task – otherwise, one suspects, many more nations would have done so. But it is difficult to assume a steady rise in the world's wealth and in technological innovations over the decades to come without also assuming that the number of nuclear powers may also increase, in rough proportion. The following is only hypothetical, but it would be a rash strategist and defense planner who did not take this possibility seriously, and quake at the implications.

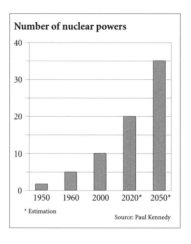

Figure 1.4

Even if the total number of nuclear states were only half that suggested here, it will be the case that the 'command control' systems of these new entrants will be ragged, and in many cases could be in the hands of regimes willing to allow their populations to take a lot of punishment, if they could also inflict punishment on the hated status quo powers. To many who study nuclear proliferation trends, it will be a miracle if humankind can get through the twenty-first century without some big bangs. Here are scenarios that make other pessimistic forecasts – for example, financial turbulence – pale by comparison.

To this concern in the arms control and armaments field can be added more. Research on, and production of, other weapons of mass destruction, for use in chemical and biological warfare, continue in many parts of the world. These are weapons that can be miniaturized and easily transported – as can, of course, miniature nuclear weapons. Moreover – and this deeply troubles established governments today

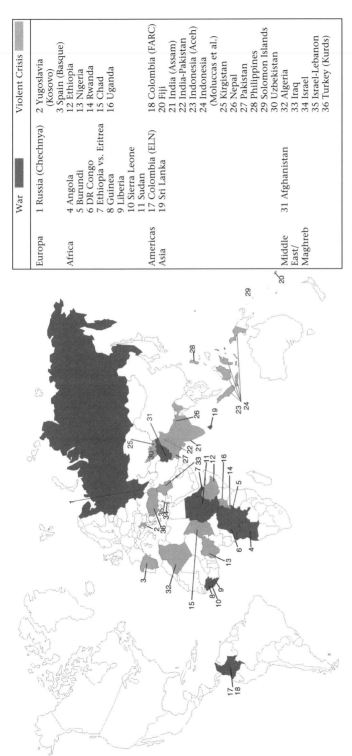

	War ▓	Violent Crisis ▓
Europa	1 Russia (Chechnya)	2 Yugoslavia (Kosovo)
		3 Spain (Basque)
Africa	4 Angola	12 Ethiopia
	5 Burundi	13 Nigeria
	6 DR Congo	14 Rwanda
	7 Ethiopia vs. Eritrea	15 Chad
	8 Guinea	16 Uganda
	9 Liberia	
	10 Sierra Leone	
	11 Sudan	
Americas	17 Colombia (ELN)	18 Colombia (FARC)
Asia	19 Sri Lanka	20 Fiji
		21 India (Assam)
		22 India-Pakistan
		23 Indonesia (Aceh)
		24 Indonesia (Moluccas et al.)
		25 Kirgistan
		26 Nepal
		27 Pakistan
		28 Philippines
		29 Solomon Islands
		30 Uzbekistan
Middle East/ Maghreb	31 Afghanistan	32 Algeria
		33 Iraq
		34 Israel
		35 Israel-Lebanon
		36 Turkey (Kurds)

Source: Heidelberg Institute for International Conflict Research 2000: Konfliktbarometer 2000. Internet document (http://www.hiik.de).

Figure 1.5

– the know-how to build such weapons, and their very transportability, make them a natural tool not only for weak states but also for non-state actors, terrorists, criminals, and ideological diehards.

Furthermore, as the military-industrial complexes of the post-Cold War world struggle with their own scaling down, they are naturally tempted to compensate by boosting sales of conventional weapons, both large and small, in any region of the world, including volatile states that are ridden with internal strife and fear external foes. In the decade or so after 1900, Krupp, Schneider-Creusot, and Vickers all poured arms into Turkey and the Balkans. Now the leading arms manufacturers of the US, Russia, and Europe, but also India, Brazil, and Israel, are pouring arms into global 'hot spots.' Even in the 1990s, the major armed conflicts occurred in regions weakened by demographic pressures, environmental stress, inadequate civil government, neglect of human rights ... plus a flourishing arms trade. How much worse might this be by 2025 or 2050? Can we learn from our history, or are we, as George Santayana suggested, condemned endlessly to repeat it?

Transborder diseases

Finally, and ironically, our sophisticated and high-tech global society faces severe challenges in the form of the oldest of dangers – disease. *Homo sapiens* has always been at war with microbes, and generally with success since the early nineteenth century (cf. McNeill 1989). But the hidden world of viruses had always probed for weaknesses, for new lines of attack. Moreover, the very expansion of human beings into hitherto uninhabited lands has exposed and unleashed new sources of disease in an ever more frequent way: mutant forms of malaria-bearing mosquitoes, resistant to the usual antidotes, Ebola from the Amazonian rainforest, Lyme disease, and hundreds more afflictions, including HIV/AIDS, which is decimating the youth of Africa and killing millions elsewhere. In June 2000, a UN agency reported that as many as half of the young men in Africa were HIV-positive.

To the inhabitants of richer societies located in temperate climes, it may seem that such epidemics are, sadly, another burden on already weakened societies in the tropics – and a long way from home. But the incidence of West Nile disease in New York, and the images of sanitation vans spraying private residences and gardens with disinfectant, is a sobering reminder that microbes and viruses recognize no boundaries. Three hundred and fifty years ago, John Donne cautioned that 'no man is an island, entire unto himself.' How much more true is that today. If the international health authorities' gloomy forecasts are even partially realized, viruses constitute a danger warranting as much attention as arms proliferation. The reports of the WHO (World Health Organization) demonstrate this.

Global trends: confusion and contradiction

As noted at the beginning of this chapter, the global trends that seem likely to be the most important over the next decades are both confusing and contradictory. Some suggest great material progress, an escape from poverty, unimaginable future standards of living, just as our standard of living in the West would be difficult for many of our grandparents to have pictured in 1950. Others suggest that the next half-century may be at least as turbulent as the years 1900–50, though perhaps in different ways.

Why the Costa Ricas of the world flourish and the Haitis flounder

A presentation such as this might well conclude with gloomy, Toynbee-esque ruminations on the human condition, on the future of world society, and the like. But this author prefers to end on a positive and a practical note. To do so, let us consider some basic data gathered by the UNDP on two very contrasting nations located in the Caribbean and Central America, namely, Haiti and Costa Rica. They have a similar climate, so that cannot explain the great differences. One has seven million inhabitants, the other around four million. Yet there are incredible contrasts in their social and economic indicators.

In every one of the indicators shown in Table 1.3, the differences are striking to an outside observer unaware of the individual circumstances. Moreover, these are chiefly data on socio-economic indicators, and do not reflect the political conditions. In addition, therefore, we should note that, whereas Costa Rica is regarded as the model democracy of Central America which has led the efforts to broker regional peace accords, Haiti is seen as a 'basket-case' with little prospect of significant political improvement.

One of the greatest contrasts between the two countries is worthy of reflection, namely, the differences in military spend and the role of the military. Haiti has too many people in uniform, whether soldiers or armed police. Its spend on the military is high, and remains a diversion from much-needed investment in the civil sector. Its government is ineffective and corrupt, and relies upon armed force. By contrast, Costa Rica has gone further perhaps than any other state in demilitarizing itself. It has abolished its army, and invites its neighbors to do the same. Its political leaders, such as Nobel Peace Prize winner Oscar Arias, speak against the arms trade and spending on weapons, whether of the large or small variety.

Table 1.3   Human Development of Costa Rica and Haiti

	Costa Rica	Haiti
Life expectancy at birth (years), 1998	76.2	54.0
Infant mortality rate (per 1,000 live births), 1998	14.0	91.0
Adult literacy rate (per cent), 1998	95.3	47.8
Military expenditures as a percentage of combined education and health expenditure, 1994	5.0	30.0
Total fertility rate (children per woman) 1995–2000	2.8	4.4
Human Development Index	0.48	150
HDI rank (total 174)	0.79	0.44

UK: HDI = 0.91; HDI rank = 10.
Source: Human Development Report 2000.

To all readers deeply interested in understanding global trends, this concern is worth taking much more seriously by our governments, whether in the rich countries that make and supply the weapons (and here, ironically, the liberal-democratic Americans are well in the lead), and in poor, corrupt, non-democratic developing states that so willingly make the purchases.

There are simple, understandable reasons why Costa Rica flourishes and Haiti flounders. It has to do with human rights, transparent government, the rule of law, appropriate investments in civil society and infrastructure, the empowerment of women, the education of girls, and freedom of expression. It has also to do with job opportunities, or the lack of them, for the millions of young people entering the job market. Will they find employment, or turn in frustration to youth armies, violence, and fundamentalist or ethnic movements? Again, the statistical data speak volumes. A country that spends a mere US$22 per head annually on healthcare but US$9,000 on each of its soldiers (as many do) shows a warped sense of priorities that is not simply immoral and offensive, but probably the single best indicator that that country is in deep trouble – or soon will be.

Three worlds of development

Will the broad mass of humanity in developing countries share the fate of Haiti by the middle of the twenty-first century, or follow Costa Rica's path? Each nation is different, but it is important to consider the overall numbers. There are 190 states on our planet, and at least 175 of them are ranked in the UNDP's annual *Human Development Report* (HDR), which, for planning purposes, divides them into three groups. The first are the prosperous, democratic, developed countries, in Europe, North America, Japan, and Australasia but joined by several others such as Israel and Singapore, and probably Chile and Argentina. They number around 30–40, depending on the 'cut-off' point one makes to the composite list.

The HDR 1997 lists 64 countries with 'high human development,' and another 65 which come in the 'medium' category. Then, at the lower end of the human development pole, there are about 50 or 60 chronically low-income countries, chiefly in Africa but also in Asia and Central America. These are the poorest of the poor. It is highly unlikely that they will be able to rescue themselves, or that private international capital flows will come to their aid. They all need help from the global community and transnational bodies, presumably orchestrated by the World Bank.

The third group, perhaps the most important for the future condition of our planet, consists of the 60–70 states that are in the middle. Like the poorest group, they face environmental, population, structural, and social challenges, but they also have educational and infrastructural resources, plus considerable (if unpredictable) access to capital. These include small nations such as Costa Rica and Jamaica, but also large, populous countries such as India, Pakistan, Brazil, Mexico, and Indonesia. If you include China, we are talking about 60 per cent of the world's population. Wherever they go, you could say, the future of the earth goes too (cf. Chase, Hill, and Kennedy 1999: Introduction and Conclusion).

These are the nations that are being globalized, modernized, brought into the world markets and world labor force at an unprecedented rate, more or less within one generation. Not surprisingly, these countries are often full of contradictions. India, for example, has the world's largest middle class – almost 200 million people – and the Bangalore region in the southeast is the second biggest producer of computer software in the world. But those 200 million middle class live alongside 750 million impoverished peasants and chronic environmental stress.

It is not an exaggeration to argue that these societies are in a race against time. Can they improve their standards of living without committing ecocide or being overwhelmed by the sheer pressure of young people in search of work? It is staggering to think that India adds to its population each year the equivalent to the total population of Australia – around 17 million. Will they all get jobs in 2020? Is this, perhaps, not the most daunting challenge of all?

Conclusion: should we be optimistic or pessimistic?

The social anthropologist's task is winding down. His ecological analysis of the planet is imperfect and incomplete, to be sure, and another scholar might describe a very different landscape than the one sketched here. But whoever steps back and attempts to survey our world as a whole is probably likely to learn that sweeping generalizations about the fate of the earth really have to be avoided. For the plain fact is that the planet on which we live is enjoying neither a new, wonderful 'world order' for everyone nor sustaining an outright disaster for all. It has great problems, but also great potential and great resources. As we enter the twenty-first century, it is easy for observers to be either too optimistic or too pessimistic, because we are looking at only one side of the story. It is particularly easy for the richer countries, which have enjoyed a near-decade of boom and an unprecedented prosperity and stock market gains, to assume all is well in the world except for some crazy people in the Balkans and Caucasia who are shooting each other.

But the planet is a lot more complicated than that. That is why we all need to take more time to study global trends and reflect on where we are going. The Chinese curse says it all: 'May you live in interesting times.' These certainly are interesting times, and are likely to become even more interesting times for our children to live in. Understanding these matters therefore is a prime prerequisite for all of us, and for our membership of the world citizenry as we advance into the twenty-first century.

A century ago H. G. Wells said that human civilization was engaged in a race between education and its own destruction. When we consider the wars and barbarism of the twentieth century, his forebodings seem uncannily accurate. Let us hope that *Homo sapiens* can get through the twenty-first century with less self-inflicted damage.

References

Chase, R., Hill, E., and Kennedy, P. (eds.) (1999) *The Pivotal States. A New Framework for U.S. Policy in the Developing World*, New York.

Connelly, M. and Kennedy, P. (1994) 'Must it be the West against the Rest?,' *The Atlantic Monthly* (December), pp. 61–84.

Hammond, A. (1998) *Which World? Scenarios for the 21st Century*, Washington, DC.

HIIK (Heidelberg Institute for International Conflict Research) (1999) *Konfliktbarometer*. <http://hiik.de>, June 7, 2001.

Human Development Report (1999) New York, p. 63.

Human Development Report (2000) New York, pp. 178–81.

Kennedy, P. (1993) *Preparing for the Twenty-First Century*, London and New York.

Landes, D. S. (1976) *The Unbound Prometheus: Technological Change and Industrial Development in Western Europe from 1750 to the Present*, London and New York.

Maddisson, A. (1995) *Monitoring the World Economy 1820–1992*, Paris.

McNeill, W. H. (1963) *The Rise of the West. A History of the Human Community*, Chicago.

McNeill, W. H. (1982) *The Pursuit of Power: Technology, Armed Force, and Society since A.D. 1000*, Chicago.

McNeill, W. H. (1989) *Plagues and Peoples*, New York.

Sivard, R. L. (1996) *World Military and Social Expenditures 1996*, Washington, DC.

Teitelbaum, M. S. and Winter, J. M. (1985) *The Fear of Population Decline*, Orlando.

UN Population Division (1998) *World Prospects: The 2000 Revision*. <http://www.un.org/esa/population/wpp2000h.pdf>, June 7, 2001.

WHO (1999) *Removing Obstacles to Healthy Development*, Geneva.

WIPO (World Intellectual Property Organization) (1998) *Program and Budget 1998–1999*. <http://www.wipo.org>, June 7, 2001.

2
World Society – Structures and Trends

Dirk Messner

The modern view of the world, which is not much more than 200 years old, reflects a revolution in thinking that took place during the process that saw the emergence of the European system of states. It was the rise of the nation-state that made it possible to view the world as a whole. In 1784 Immanuel Kant coined the term 'cosmopolitan society,' giving it precise shape in his essay 'On Perpetual Peace' (1795). By 1740 French freemason texts were describing the world as a great republic embracing every nation as a family and each individual as its child. Schlegel (1802) and Goethe (1827) were the first to speak of world literature. World exhibitions have been a more or less regular occurrence since 1851. In 1858 the first transatlantic cable was laid; in 1869 the Suez Canal was opened; in 1874 the Universal Postal Union was founded – transportation and communications began to link one continent to another, opening up the world.

The first half of the twentieth century was marked by two world wars and a worldwide economic crisis. The first photographs of the 'blue planet,' made possible by manned space travel in the 1960s, translated into a picture of 'One World.' In the 1990s the Commission for Global Governance presented its report 'Our Global Neighborhood,' a model of the organization of modern life in the 'Global Village.' As the twentieth century drew to a close, the epoch of the nation-state was being supplanted by the epoch of globalism.

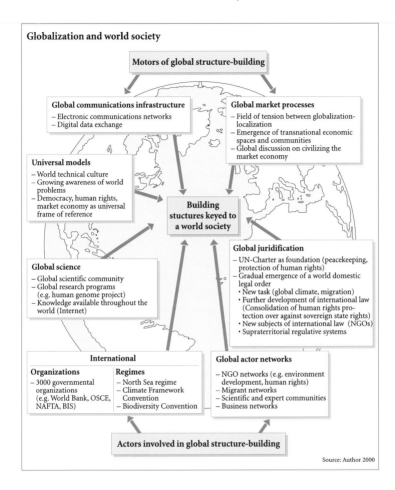

Figure 2.1

The international community is successively developing in the direction of a world society.

World society: reality or phantom?

The process of globalization that we have experienced in recent decades has accelerated the coalescence of the world. Boundaries that for centuries divided one national society from another are becoming increasingly porous. Global spaces, interdependencies, and trends are transforming societies, economies, and even individuals' reference systems:

- The Chernobyl disaster of 1986 and the hole in the ozone layer detected in the 1990s have made it starkly clear that humanity as a whole is growing into a *global risk community.*
- Globalization of the international financial markets, underway since the breakdown of the Bretton Woods system in 1973, is accelerating the formation of a *global market economy* which, since the collapse of the socialist bloc at the end of the 1980s, has become the frame of reference for the development efforts undertaken by most of the world's economies.
- The Internet revolution, underway only since the mid-1990s, is building entirely new foundations for a *worldwide communications and knowledge infrastructure,* which is profoundly altering economies, sciences, consumption patterns, and individual and cultural relations.
- Intercontinental air travel, just a few decades ago a luxury good for the few, has become a mass commodity, at least in the industrialized countries. It is an indication of the emergence of a *world-embracing transportation and traffic infrastructure* conveying transnational flows of goods, tourists, and migrants.

World society: a controversial concept

The use of the term 'world' in composites is largely uncontroversial: 'world economy,' 'world ecology,' and 'world peace' have taken their place in our everyday language. By contrast, the term 'world society,' introduced into the debate in 1972 by John Burton, remains contentious. In essence, four arguments are advanced to disprove the thesis that we are witnessing the emergence of a 'world society' (Altvater and Mahnkopf 1996; Czempiel 1981):

- A 'society' presupposes a minimum consensus and is the outcome of an explicit or implicit social contract. These conditions do not obtain in the global context.
- In the absence of social equality and comparable living conditions it is unlikely that a social contract could emerge or take on a concrete and stable shape. In global terms, however, the first and most striking thing we encounter is the enormous disparities between rich and poor countries with the highly

divergent technological and socioeconomic development levels associated with them.

- Social contracts presuppose the existence of a minimum of 'we-sentiments' (Elias) and cultural commonalities. Throughout the world, however, we can observe hundreds of different ethnic groups, a plurality of cultures, and hence also a diversity of societies: factors seemingly working counter to the development of a 'world society.'
- Societies are governed or ruled by states. A 'world society,' it is claimed, would thus presuppose a 'world state.'

These arguments are based on the transference of the characteristics of national societies to the world as a whole, that is, of a specific type of society that emerged in the 'epoch of the nation-state.' World society is thus, as it were, conceived as a national society magnified to the global scale – and for this reason regarded as an impossibility. This view inhibits our understanding of the profound changes that are underway in national societies as well as of the new social processes and the emergent structures for which globalization is responsible.

On the one hand, at the end of the twentieth century the societies found in many nation-states no longer corresponded to the traditional picture of society either. It is not only 'world society' that is marked by deep social disparities, they are no less characteristic of many national societies. The life expectancy of young blacks in many US inner cities is certainly no greater than that for youths in many of the poorest countries in Asia and Africa. In 1993 President Clinton, in a speech on the problems facing inner cities in the US, rightly warned of the danger that the underclass could turn into an 'outer class.' Moreover, in cultural terms, many national societies are characterized by growing heterogeneity, due to historical factors or to immigration. World-views and life-worlds are also becoming increasingly differentiated, a development that is leading to the erosion of the classical mechanisms of social integration, which operate through shared values, religion, or membership in relatively stable social milieux. This is why, at the threshold to the twenty-first century, the search is underway in many national societies for the stuff from which new social contracts can be fashioned. There are many indications that globalization-related trends will continue to lead to further social and cultural heterogeneity in national societies.

On the other hand, against the background of the analyses presented by *Global Trends*, there are good reasons for the argument that globalization fosters processes that seem to be moving in the direction of a world society. If what we understand by society is (in keeping with the sociological and politico-logical definitions currently in use) the 'most comprehensive system of human community' or the 'social system of the highest order' (Talcott Parsons), then it is logical to speak in the narrower sense of national societies and in the broader sense of a developing world society. The border-crossing dynamics and dimensions of many functional systems of society (e.g. the economy, environment, law, science, the military), inter- and transnational interdependencies, intertwined multilevel politics extending from the local to the global, the growing worldwide acceptance of uniform standards, norms, values, and patterns of regulation, regional integration processes, and the emergence of global players (world corporations, e.g. Daimler Chrysler; NGOs such as Greenpeace) are leading to the creation of new structures that can no longer be modeled on the concept of the '*inter*national system.' The changes outlined make it plain that in many areas national societies no longer constitute the 'most comprehensive system of human community.'

Ernst-Otto Czempiel (1993: 106f.) is right in noting that the world 'is not yet a world society, though it is no longer a world of nation-states either.' Yet the growing consolidation of 'global trends' is gradually leading to the formation of a world society – and such a formation will be a social order (a society) that differs qualitatively from national societies. It will continue to present alternatives – at the local or national level, in different regions or continents, e.g. as regards the final shape given to concrete production relations, cultural patterns, systems of social and environmental regulation, and ways of life. Nor will national societies vanish, though they will be bound up in increasingly densely networked relations deriving from the emerging world society, and will likewise change in the process. In view of the dynamics of 'global trends' and interdependencies, there is no longer any alternative to a functionally differentiated and increasingly more densely networked world society which unfolds a development dynamics of its own and is more than the sum of nation-states and their mutual relations.

This analysis is in line with the view of the German 'Research Group World Society' [*Forschungsgruppe Weltgesellschaft*] (1996). The authors describe the points of transition from the international system to an international society, pointing to development trends working in the direction of a world society. The international society differs from the international system in terms of its higher degree of organization. Common rules, institutions, and dialogue structures here are placing the relations between states on a qualitatively new footing (Buzan 1993). The emerging new world society is based on the increasing involvement of non-statal actors in transboundary interactions as well as on a multiplication and networking of political, economic, and social levels of action.

International system	*Interrelation* of and *interaction* between states.
International society	*In addition: institutionalization processes* Institutionalized rules of conduct for states, based on common interests. Intensification of systematic international relations with the common goal of developing norms and institutions (international organizations, regimes). Stabilization of expectations by establishing rules governing international relations.
World society	*In addition: diversification and diffusion of actors, further differentiation of action levels, stabilization of universal guiding principles* Apart from states, economic and social actors are becoming global players in world politics. Transnational spaces are emerging. Local, national, regional, and global levels of action are more and more densely interwoven. Universal guiding principles are in the process of being established.

Source: *Forschungsgruppe Weltgesellschaft* 1996: 18 (modified).

The epoch of the nation-state

The 'epoch of the nation-state' began with the Peace of Westphalia of 1648, which created a system of independent nation-states. 'The nation,' conceived as a political entity, and the sovereign nation-state, capable of shaping and articulating social life within its territorial boundaries, are an 'invention' of the eighteenth and nineteenth centuries. The models for the democratic state under the rule of law and the mass democracy anchored in the welfare state are products of the nineteenth and twentieth centuries. It was above all the OECD countries that sought orientation in them after 1945. But most developing countries and, since 1989, the former socialist states have embraced democracy organized along the lines of the nation-state and a socially restrained market economy as at least target systems of their development efforts.

In other words, the nation-state, the crucial and pivotal point of modern political thought, is a comparatively recent historical product, one that emerged in and through processes fraught with conflict. In Europe, the number of politically independent entities declined from 500 to 25 between 1500 and 1900. The modern nation-states developed at the expense of the power of the estates (clergy, nobility, towns), which had been dominant since the thirteenth century. The means leading to the emergence of the modern nation-state included the concentration of the means of military power, territorial amalgamation, standardization of legal systems, creation of financial systems independent of the ruling princes, and abolition of internal customs tariffs as a means of creating unified economic spaces. Even at the beginning of the eighteenth century there were still some 1,800 customs frontiers across the German territories. The German *Zollverein* (tariff union), established in 1833, gradually brought most of the German territories together to form a unified economic area.

With a few exceptions, such as in England and the Netherlands, this process initially gave rise to systems of absolutist rule. It is only from the mid-nineteenth century that we find a transition to constitutional regimes and the domestication of the state's unfettered power to act which the former imply. The territorial state, the nation as a polity, and self-determination as regards the organization of social life within national boundaries (sovereignty) characterize the historical constellation in which democracy found its place and – at least in the western industrialized states – progress was made in restraining the forces of the market economy by introducing elements of the social welfare state. This process saw the nation-states assume the role of organizational centers of social life, politics, and social integration. The nation-states were the setting in which the complex institutional arrangements arose that have subsequently been used for purposes of national conflict management and social integration. The internal consolidation of the nation-states went hand in hand with newly developing relations between them. It is only at the end of the eighteenth century that terms such as 'international' and 'international relations' became common parlance. In the 'epoch of the nation-state' the world was constituted as a 'world of states.'

Globalization and the contours of a 'post-national constellation'

The term 'globalization' made its first appearance in an English-language reference work in 1961. Since the 1980s the term has become a core concept in scholarly and political debate, one that reflects incisive changes in the real world. Instead of describing a final state, globalization denotes a process in the course of which the volume and intensity of transboundary transportation, communication, and trade relations are rapidly increasing. It is undermining the divisive connotations of national boundaries, and intensifying the impacts of border-crossing economic, social, and political activities for national societies. Many pressing problems cut across territorial boundaries, more and more events are simultaneously perceived throughout the world, making themselves felt, with increasingly brief delays, in more and more places. This entails shifts in the way we understand politics and the demands we place on it.

While in the epoch of the nation-state international politics was concerned with 'external' events, today global developments extend into national societies in different ways. The boundaries between domestic and foreign policy are becoming blurred (Messner 1998). Discussions over the question of 'one world,' 'world ethics,' 'earth politics,' 'world domestic policy,' 'mankind as a global risk community,' or 'global governance' indicate the direction in which this process of change is taking us.

In the nineteenth century the railroad, steam navigation, and the telegraph accelerated the conveyance of goods and people and the exchange of information. At the end of the twentieth century it was satellite technology, the Internet, and air transportation that were revolutionizing and globalizing the exchange processes between

people, technology, and nature. Networked telecommunication is
the most effective infrastructure in this process. Via the Internet,
news, images, money, and knowledge move at previously unprecedented speed in virtual space, engendering worldwide effects – in
real space.

The analyses presented by *Global Trends* make it clear that it would
be mistaken to reduce globalization solely to economic processes.
The analyses indicate instead an international diffusion of mass
tourism, mass culture, telecommunication infrastructure, science,
and transportation systems. The risks posed by new technologies
(e.g. reproductive and genetic technologies) or by weapons systems
are of a transnational and often global nature. The patterns of
production and consumption gaining prevalence throughout the
world are causing local environmental problems, though it is above
all the global ecosystems that they threaten to overburden to
disastrous effect. Many NGOs, as well as communities of scientists
and experts, the media, and associations, have for some years been
engaged in the role of global players, keeping step, albeit belatedly,
with the process of economic globalization.

Different ways in which global structures are formed

Transnational interaction between actors. *Global Trends*
points to five types of transnational interaction patterns
between actors in a global governance architecture: interactions
(1) between states (intergovernmental cooperation); (2) between
states and private actors (new forms of public/private partnership), e.g. in the context of human rights protection and the
drafting of codes of conduct for the tourism industry; (3)
without states (governance without government), e.g. in the
framework of ISO standards in the world economy or negotiation of codes of conduct by multinational corporations and
NGOs; (4) in the context of the over 100 existing regional integration projects (regional governance); (5) between existing
regional integration projects, e.g. in the field of trade between
the EU and MERCOSUR.

Concatenated global interdependencies. *Negative global chains
of interdependence*: International financial crises (e.g. the Asia
crisis) have worldwide impacts, trigger employment crises,

growth-inhibiting debt spirals, impoverishment, and social tensions, can lead to waves of migration and provoke export-dumping and protectionism. *Positive chains of interdependence*: Investment made in multinational corporations in developing countries can spark positive growth and employment effects, accelerate transnational technology transfer, contribute to the acceptance of progressive environmental and social standards, and give rise to cooperative efforts on the part of NGOs and labor unions in the home and target countries of investors.

Integration processes in the course of globalization. We can observe a great variety of border-crossing integration processes: countries joining forces to form regional integration projects; business integration aimed at forming transnational corporations; scientists founding worldwide associations; the emergence of global interest organizations (labor unions, business federations, environmental organizations).

Processes of interpenetration in the course of globalization. Economic globalization, the exchange of news, knowledge, images, and other cultural goods via the global communications infrastructure and the phenomenon of worldwide tourism tend to promote mutual interpenetration of and interaction between cultures and cultural models. One of the effects of international joint ventures between companies as well as of various forms of coordination and cooperation between the different levels of action of the global governance architecture is that actor orientations and modes of action are mutually intertwined, influenced, altered, and reconstituted across international borders.

These processes go far beyond the accustomed national perspective in terms of which politics, business, and science have interpreted the world for centuries. An increasing number of social subsystems are growing beyond national boundaries and the regulatory systems contained in them (Zürn 1998). These are the building blocks, elements, and fragments of an emerging world society. Globalization overcomes and breaks down national borders, opening up new options for businesses, organizations, and individuals, while at the same time, and in many different ways, restricting the scope of action of nation-states and threatening certain forms of social integration anchored in the (national) welfare state. Because thus far democracy and the rule of law have been realized credibly and effectively only in the national framework, the 'post-national constellation' (Habermas 1998) is also shaking the foundations on which the concept of democratic government rests.

Globalization, a Janus-faced phenomenon

Just as the dynamism informing the process that led to the formation of the nation-state in essence first made itself felt in the cities and the trade and traffic between them, spurred on by the invention of printing, globalization likewise does not impact on all spheres of society and groups of actors at the same time or with the same force (Gummet 1996). The market mechanisms dominant throughout the world following the collapse of socialism – in particular financial markets, globally active corporations, and technical upheavals in the fields of information and communications technology – are the motors of globalization.

The driving forces of globalization are placing all societies under pressure to adjust, though these should not be equated with processes of homogenization. Growing inter- and transnational interdependencies, processes of networking, standardization, and adaptation are leading to new forms of integration in a newly emerging world society. These are set against disintegration tendencies (see the box 'Paradoxes of Modernization Processes in World Society,' below). Janus-faced globalization gives rise to new forms of:

- *Exclusion*: for instance, workers in uncompetitive firms, entire countries marginalized in the global economy, governments that lose access to the global financial markets on account of their high debt levels.
- *Fragmentation*: for instance, due to the coexistence of 'flourishing' regions and regions unable to cope with the demands of the world market; the simultaneous existence of modern, western-oriented, globally networked urban elites and 'decoupled' rural population groups in many developing countries.
- *Asynchronisms*: for instance, due to globalized markets that still lack institutional political structures or in view of the unlimited

potentials of the Internet which, in many developing countries, run up against an infrastructure in which the telephone is still a luxury good. Another striking aspect is the simultaneous existence of different types of nation-states. The first are those that respond to globalization by organizing regional integration projects, sharing some of their sovereignty with other states and developing new forms of statehood; the second are those that are still in the phase of nation-building and seek their orientation in the model of the 'strong nation-state' (e.g. India, Russia) seeking to safeguard its independence in a globalized world; the third group includes numerous cases of state disintegration (e.g. Rwanda, Columbia, the Balkan states).

The development of world society is, therefore, a process that is neither linear nor in itself conducive to peace or social integration. Imbedding globalization processes in a cooperation-oriented global governance architecture is therefore one of the tasks facing the twenty-first century. One central problem is that world society will be forced to get along without the forms of political, social, and normative integration long characteristic of the nation-state, a fact rightly pointed to by critics of the idea of a world society. How can a minimum of social balance be established in the global context? What shape might a global minimal ethics have that, looking beyond the confines of the nation-state, seeks to strengthen 'we-sentiments' and foster a sense of global responsibility? How can global competition be harmonized with a transnational culture of cooperation aimed at dealing effectively with world problems? In what form is democracy conceivable beyond the nation-state? These are some of the fundamental questions that are raised by globalization and have prompted Ralf Dahrendorf to warn of an 'authoritarian century.'

The political, social, and institutional shape that world society may take in the future is still an open question. *De facto*, the world is proving more and more to be a common life-world of people calling for universally binding rules based on human rights and social justice (see Figure 2.2). Yet the political, institutional, legal, and moral institutions of society remain more attuned to the 'epoch of the nation-state,' a fact that stands in the way of any attempt to temper the dynamics inherent in globalization processes. Richard Falk rightly emphasizes that thus far we have been faced with a

Paradoxes of modernization processes in world society

1. The *paradox of instrumental activism*: Every intervention in the world (whether technological, political, or legal) entails a variety of consequences and secondary effects as well as interdependencies which run counter to the intended purpose and other aims. We are living in the age of the secondary effect.
2. The *paradox of rationalism*: The growth of our knowledge is accompanied by a proportionate, indeed disproportionate, knowledge of our ignorance, because every new scientific discovery abruptly illuminates unexplored terrains, casting doubt on what was thought to be secure knowledge.
3. The *paradox of individualism*: Enlargement of the individual's options and scope of action is accompanied by an increase in the number of people on whose decisions the success of the individual's actions depend. More freedom at the same time engenders more constraints.
4. The *paradox of universalism*: Equality achieved in one place engenders inequalities in other places. Improved educational opportunities in the OECD countries have, for instance, for some of the lower and the lower middle class, opened the way into the upper middle class while at the same time intensifying the competition for better positions, in this way all the more sharply marginalizing the less competitive with fewer or no educational qualifications and generating new social problems.

Source: Münch 1998: 21.

'market- oriented globalism' and that the great challenge facing us today is to set the stage for a 'people-oriented globalism.'

The great challenge of the twenty-first century: civilizing the global market economy

The world faces a paradox: globalization is creating more and more options and fields of action for organizations, businesses, and individuals. Never before have so many people been so mobile, so well

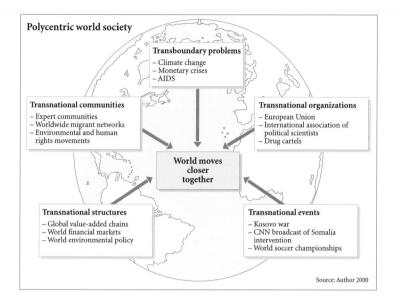

Polycentric world society

Transboundary problems
– Climate change
– Monetary crises
– AIDS

Transnational communities
– Expert communities
– Worldwide migrant networks
– Environmental and human
  rights movements

Transnational organizations
– European Union
– International association of
  political scientists
– Drug cartels

**World moves
closer
together**

Transnational structures
– Global value-added chains
– World financial markets
– World environmental policy

Transnational events
– Kosovo war
– CNN broadcast of Somalia
  intervention
– World soccer championships

Source: Author 2000

Figure 2.2

informed, and so closely tied to transboundary social, economic, cultural, and political networks. At the same time, actors seem to be losing their capacity to reach a collective understanding on how they want to live and organize their societies. Opportunities and welfare gains seem to correlate with a decrease of political governance capacity:

- Multinational corporations can boost the economic dynamism of the regions in which they invest. Yet at the same time global mobility undercuts the ability of nation-states to prevent their social, environmental, or collective bargaining systems from being undermined and eroded. Even a threat to relocate has – as the case of Germany *inter alia* demonstrates – a disciplinary effect on governments.
- Global information and communications networks make possible accelerated learning processes and a cost-effective diffusion of knowledge throughout the world, though they may also serve as infrastructure for organized crime or political and religious extremists.
- The global diffusion of scientific-technical civilization is rapidly leading to the innovation dynamics required to solve

the world's most pressing social and ecological problems, though this development also raises ethical questions of hitherto unknown magnitudes (e.g. in genetic and reproductive technology) and gives rise to technological hazards that cannot be mastered within the boundaries of the nation-state and yet still resist resolution beyond its borders.

- Organized global mass culture, while free of the narrowness and limitations of local folklore, nevertheless tends to reproduce a shallow and trivial culture and threatens to crush the diversity of the world's cultures.
- The balance of political power between mobile actors (e.g. businesses, owners of capital, highly qualified workers) able to evade the constraints of national borders, regulatory systems, and sanctions and immobile actors (e.g. states, governments, labor unions, political parties) is disrupted.

The list of the opportunities and risks of globalization could be extended against the backdrop of the analyses presented by *Global Trends* (see 'Problem Types Involved in Globalization,' below). Transnational problem constellations and border-crossing conflict complexes can contribute to the development of new forms of intra- and supranational cooperation and problem-solving, though they may also give rise to new distributional conflicts. The analyses presented by *Global Trends* provide graphic illustrations for both lines of development.

Because markets, actors, and problem complexes increasingly extend beyond national boundaries, we are confronted once again, at both the global and the national levels, with problems that dogged welfare state democracies at the national level. As the world coalesces, many questions are returning that were given shape by the early phase of capitalism. After the Second World War, capitalism was largely civilized within the national framework, at least in the western industrialized countries; one task high on today's agenda is to civilize the global market economy. How, in the 'epoch of globalism,' is it possible to harness the dynamics and the allocative and discovery functions of markets more effectively without losing sight of the need to come to terms with the new transboundary economic, ecological, and cultural risks? In what form can the civilizing achievements of the liberal constitutional state and the social-integrative accomplishments of the welfare state be safeguarded in the context of a global governance architecture? What role will the nation-state have in the future?

The nation-state in the 'epoch of globalism'

The physiognomy of the world of states is changing irreversibly. The key notions of the sovereign state and the sacrosanct national community, still dominant in international politics, are lagging behind the reality created by globalization. Societies are coalescing to form a worldwide system of interdependence. The 'epoch of the nation-state' appears to be giving way to an 'epoch of globalism.' This transition is accompanied, and accelerated, by the transformation of societies from industrial societies into information and knowledge societies, the diminishing significance of distances and territorial boundaries, and a multiplication of inter-, supra-, and transnational actors and organizations that are joining the nation-states as active subjects on the stage of international affairs. Nation-states, for the last two centuries the centers of societies and the main actors in international politics, will have to adjust to the new challenges if they are not to lose control of the centrifugal forces and the dynamics generated by globalism.

The analyses presented by *Global Trends* clearly indicate that states need not be the losers of globalization, though their role is undergoing radical change. Four trends can be observed here:

1. Workable supranational regulatory systems are based on functioning national institutions, which means that globalization is contributing not to the extinction but to the transformation of politics at the level of the nation-state. No viable global governance architecture can come about without strong and effective nation-states.

2. Transboundary processes and dynamics have very different effects on the governance capacity of different nation-states. Thus, for instance, as far as the field of economic policy is concerned, we see that there is considerable scope for potential action in the field of technology and innovation policies, while international cooperation, regulation, and indeed, in some cases, harmonization are becoming increasingly important in the fields of monetary, currency, and financial policy as a means of preventing global instabilities. In other fields too we see that the action potentials of the nation-state vary sharply from problem complex to problem complex, though these potentials show no signs of linear decline.

Problem types involved in globalization

1. **Global goods** (and bads)
   - Protection of the international climate
   - Protection of biodiversity
   - Protection of the ozone layer
   - Stability of the international financial system, etc.

2. **Transboundary problems**
   - Migration
   - Pollution of the seas
   - Acid rain
   - Corruption, etc.

3. **Global phenomena**
   - Mega-cities
   - Crisis faced by large-scale hierarchical organizations
   - Employment crises, etc.

4. **Global interdependence – problems**
   - Economic crises – immiseration processes – migration
   - World trade – transportation – ecological costs of mobility
   - Declining growth in industrialized countries – declining energy consumption – employment problems in North and South alike

5. **System competition (locational competition)**
   - Downward spiraling races to cut taxes
   - (Cost) competition between systems of social and environmental regulation
   - Erosion of the social and ecological dimensions of the market economy, etc.

6. **Complexity of global governance architecture**
   - Deficits in democracy and legitimacy
   - Coordination problems posed by a multilevel politics
   - Risk of bargaining blockades
   - Blockades due to asymmetrical power structures, etc.

---

3. All problem fields are seeing new forms of policy-making develop in an emerging global governance architecture. At the end of the twentieth century a multilevel policy entailing increasingly

densely networked local, national, regional, and global policies has proved to be the rule (Young 1997).

4. Globalization does not contribute necessarily to the erosion of national action potentials but may give rise to incentive structures that promote democratization, decentralization, international cooperation, and a greater measure effectiveness and efficiency of state action:

- *Nation-states are becoming internationally accountable*: New international legal norms, institutions, and regimes are curtailing the dominance of the nation-state in some important areas (human rights, the environment, social standards) and establishing minimum standards valid throughout the world. Processes of international juridification are leading to a situation in which government legitimacy is increasingly measured in terms of international rules and standards.
- *Democratization and the process of civilizing the market economy can be effectively supported 'from outside'*: International NGOs have – thanks not least to the global communications infrastructure – been intervening more and more directly in 'national' policy processes in the fields of human rights, the environment, development, and welfare.
- *Nation-states are coming under growing pressure to increase their effectiveness and efficiency*: Throughout the world countries are confronted with social groups pointing to international agreements, conventions, and experience (e.g. the Agenda 21 processes) and calling for improved government services, functioning regulatory systems, and participation.
- *Economic globalization is strengthening decentralization processes in nation-states and regional cooperation in world regions*: In the context of the world economy central governments are coming under pressure from their regions, which are keen to promote their profiles in global competition. For developing countries in particular, this opens up the opportunity to bring politics closer to the people. At the same time, globalization is accelerating processes of regional economic and political cooperation in all areas of the world, a project that in the past failed repeatedly in the

face of narrow-minded national concerns. Experiences from the OECD countries show that economic and political integration can contribute to the creation of zones of peace.

Building structures keyed to world society

Today, we cannot yet predict what form the emerging world society will take. It is, though, possible to point to some important areas in which the structure-building processes aimed at a world society are already underway and to indicate what new lines of conflict will mark world society in the twenty-first century.

Motors of global structure-building; technology and the market

Global communications infrastructure

Satellites, information technology, and the Internet are developing into a global communications infrastructure in which space and time have practically ceased to be barriers. This is giving rise to the conditions of a process of worldwide networking in the economy and society and leading to the globalization of the media. Just as public infrastructure in the form of energy systems, roads, and railroads created the potential for the factories of the first and second industrial revolutions, electronic communications networks and digital information exchange are becoming the motor of the third industrial revolution as well as of economic globalization. The all-important innovation implied by this infrastructure, with its electronic networks and data transmission lines, is that it facilitates communications unbound by the territoriality, making it possible to find, exchange, and use information rapidly and cost-efficiently. This 'intelligent infrastructure' will be a key factor of economic competitiveness in the knowledge-based economies of the twenty-first century.

The communications revolution is at the same time revolutionizing the structures of social relations, the dynamics of science, and the learning capacities of organizations and societies. NGOs have proved to be highly innovative in making use of the Internet as a platform for democratic information and action. On the whole, all areas of society are affected by the rapid growth in the volume and the geographic reach of information-processing technologies and the means of their diffusion.

Objections to the concept of a world state

Some authors look to the model of a world state as an adequate response to the phenomenon of globalization. There are some good objections to this centralist concept (Höffe 1998, pp. 210f.):

1. Conflicts in the emerging world society (e.g. territorial conflicts, demands for self-determination, environmental conflicts) would not be solved but merely transformed from international conflicts into domestic conflicts. A global state would have three further disadvantages: a) any elimination of state boundaries would lower significant thresholds to warlike conflicts; b) a borderless world would eliminate any chance of flight and exile; c) a world state would be without the option of exerting outside pressure to bring down a dictatorship.
2. A global state would be remote from its citizens, excessively bureaucratic, and, thanks to its size and convoluted makeup, incapable of solving complex problems. Moreover, once borders had disappeared, competition between states, constitutions, and different institutional designs would be lost, and with them important motors of social creativity and progress in development.
3. A global state would be all but incapable of protecting social and cultural diversity, since any such cultural heterogeneity would necessarily lead such a state to seek greater homogenization. Immanuel Kant warned of the 'soulless despotism' of a world state, which would run the risk of becoming the 'graveyard of freedom.' This argument finds echoes in Michael Walzer's warning of the 'cosmopolitan communitarian.' Walzer emphasizes that 'good fences' are the basis of 'just societies' and viable forms of transboundary cooperation.
4. The road from a world of sovereign, competing states to a world state would hardly be a peaceful one, and the imperative of international conflict prevention would consequently rule out this approach from the very start.

The US has pioneered this revolution. In 1993, the Clinton administration made the development of a 'global information infrastructure' one of the priorities of its term of office. In the US the number of data connections made in 1995 for the first time outnumbered the number of telephone calls placed; the number of computers sold for the first time exceeded the figures for TV sales; the number of e-mails for the first time outnumbered the number of letters conveyed by the Postal Service. In the 1990s Japan and Europe likewise made enormous investments in communications infrastructure in an attempt to catch up with the US (Seitz 1998). The countries of the South are engaged in a process of infrastructure development that is progressing at a far slower pace. Nevertheless, the new technologies do offer the poorer countries real opportunities, as well as risks, in that these technologies, compared with fax and telephone, open up new, fast, and cost-effective avenues of knowledge-transfer. Many small and medium-sized businesses, as well as many scientists and NGOs in developing countries, are seizing this new possibility to communicate on a worldwide basis.

Global structure-building via market processes

Global market mechanisms, financial flows, and technological development dynamics are the elements that go into the making of the world economy, though these same elements are also leading to the formation of a multiplicity of structures that point in the direction of a world society. International competitiveness, whether of businesses or of regions, determines employment levels and thus purchasing power, consumption patterns, political attitudes, the elements of social conflict, etc. The world market extends into national societies, and local and national actors, businesses, and institutions are, therefore, increasingly forced to keep track of international technological, organizational, and social developments with a view to being able to come up with viable action strategies. The alternative to passive adjustment to the conditions of the world market is active, transnational learning, working together with global players, building specific profiles and systemic competitive advantages, so seeking to play a major role in shaping global trends.

Because competitiveness is based on both business competitiveness and the institutional setting in which businesses operate (e.g. systems of education/training, technology, infrastructure, taxation, environmental regulation), economic globalization is also forcing political institutions to seek orientation in the frame of reference defined by the world market (Messner 1997). This leads to new forms of transboundary competition and to more international cooperation and coordination among political institutions, for instance in the framework of regional integration projects like the EU or MERCOSUR. In other words, it is less and less possible to reduce social processes to national causes, since they are increasingly the product of transnational framework conditions. Economic globalization thus entails the integration of non-economic actors into the structures of transnational relations. More and more functional social systems are emerging from the straitjacket imposed by the nation-state.

Economic globalization is leading to the formation of three different types of structure which are changing the face of the emerging world society:

1. The relation between *globalization and localization* is one of mutual reinforcement. In the context of the world market local, location-specific competitive advantages, and thus local actors and institutions, are gaining importance – with those actors proving most successful that seek integration in transboundary learning partnerships.

2. We can observe that market globalization leads to the emergence of *transnational economic spaces and communities*. When leading German financial and banking actors begin to regard their dealings with global stock exchanges, fund, and issuing establishments as more important than their relations defined under national monetary policy, i.e. by the Bundesbank, national funds, and issuing agencies, then we can speak of the emergence of a lateral world financial system. And when important German businesses and associations successively begin to see their relations with institutions of the economic Triad (the EU, US, Japan) as important as those which they entertain with German policy-making institutions or the German R&D system, then we can say that institutional structures once based on formerly national foundations are being transformed into transnational actor systems (transnational elites).

3. The discussions surrounding international social and environmental standards show that globalization of the economy directly entails a *globalization of the discourses and political debates concerning the possibility of civilizing the market economy*. One striking fact is that these processes have been set in train by

globally active NGOs – and not, say, by labor unions or states. More and more frequently NGOs are entering into direct negotiations with multilateral corporations. Their aim in doing so is to push through higher social and environmental standards in the corporations in question and their suppliers. Big corporations such as Shell, Levis, and Nike have been forced to make concessions in these discussions in order to avoid tarnishing their image. In other words, what we are seeing here is the emergence of new forms of transnational private governance (governance without government).

Political actors of world society

International organizations and regimes

International organizations, regimes, and conventions are indicators of the strong interdependence between states reliant in many problem fields on cooperative strategies and collective solutions if they are to avoid the deleterious consequences of uncoordinated action and attain common goals. Some 3,000 international organizations constitute the building blocks of the 'era of globalism,' and it is in them that successive global perceptions and policy approaches can develop which are no longer tied directly to national interests. The international organizations developed in recent years are of an entirely different character. We need think here only of 'program organizations' such as the OSCE or the Council of Europe, 'forum organizations' such as the UN General Assembly, 'service organizations' such as the FAO and WHO, and 'control institutions' such as the BIS or the IMF.

International regimes, which have been gaining in importance since the 1980s and which see states committing themselves by treaty to contribute to jointly processing common problems (e.g. the North Sea regime, Climate Framework Convention, Biodiversity Convention), constitute innovative elements of the emerging global governance architecture (see this volume, Chapter 4). The regional integration projects which grew in importance in the 1990s (see this volume, Chapter 3) are leading to the formation of inter- and supranational institutional structures. Regional governance is becoming a core element of the global governance architecture. It is because inter- and supranational organizations and regimes are more and more closely interlinked with NGOs, communities of scientists, multilateral corporations, or municipalities that they are becoming points of departure for the building of new international structures.

Global networks

Transnational networks of private actors, which are intervening more and more actively in the work of international governmental organizations, constitute the humus from which a global civil society could emerge. International labor federations, global networks of environmental and human rights organizations, internationally active associations of scientists, experts, and lobbyists, as well as transboundary migrant networks, and, not least, globally operating entrepreneurial organizations are developing in directions at odds with the established structures of the international system. In recent decades networks of civil society actors have shown their ability to act globally. It is to their persistence that we owe, for instance, the convention banning the use of anti-personnel mines and the first steps on the road toward an International Criminal Court.

Beyond the nation-state, classical international politics and diplomacy, local, national, and global behavior patterns, cultures, and interests come together in inter- and transnational networks. New political spaces are emerging in which, beyond diplomatic channels, common search and learning processes, creative problem-solving patterns, and transboundary modes of interest coordination are being developed, though these spaces can also, and at the same time, constitute arenas in which conflicts may develop and flare up. The follow-up processes to the major world conferences have become points of departure for this trend. The great number of actors involved indicates that there is hardly a social, economic, or cultural area that is excluded from these world-embracing communication networks.

Moreover, it is only recently that international organizations as well as private actors and networks have begun to initiate and engage in close cooperation. The active involvement of many NGOs in the world conferences in recent years and the opening of the World Bank to NGOs, for instance in the form of institutionalized consulting procedures in connection with evaluating the social impacts of structural adjustment, point in this direction. One leading example of new forms of 'public/private partnership' in international relations is the attempt, initiated in 1998 by UNDP and other UN organizations, to cooperate with multinational corporations with a view to moving them to commit themselves to protect international

human rights and help to introduce minimum social and environmental standards in their organizations as well as in the world
economy, the aim being to push for realization of the goal of a
'global market with a human face.'

Universal models

One factor that characterizes the emerging world society is the
diversity of its cultures and the intricate plurality of its norms and
value systems. Nevertheless, worldwide we cannot fail to observe a
striking standardization of cognitive patterns in critical areas.

1. The course of the modern age has seen the rise of a 'world
    technical culture' based on uniform calendars, standards for
    measures, weights, and money, and a secular world-view.
2. Globalization and world problems are giving rise to a growing
    'world consciousness' that finds expression *inter alia* in the search
    for viable world environmental policies or global human rights
    institutions. Agenda 21 is a crystallization point in this process.
3. The basic institutions of economy and society at the end of the
    twentieth century – in contrast to the situation dominant just a
    few years earlier – were marked worldwide by a broad consensus:
    democracy, human rights, and the market economy have gained
    prevalence as universal models – even though it must be noted
    that they are still far from being fully realized and stabilized.

Universalization should not be confused with homogenization. It is
precisely the consolidation of worldwide relations that has stoked
international debates on different human rights concepts and the
conditions needed to give a promising shape to democracy and
market economy. Accordingly, it is the widening consensus on the
underlying structures of development and the global diffusion of the
core elements of modernity that are simultaneously generating
intensified conflicts on how, specifically, democracy, human rights,
and market economy are to be understood. In a segmented world,
border-crossing controversies over the meaning of 'universal models'
would be superfluous. In the emerging world society these often
conflict-laden communication processes over common foundations
for 'one world' and the specifics of spontaneously grown local and
national cultures are necessary and inevitable.

The universalization of cognitive patterns is, on the one hand,
accelerated by the media and world-embracing communications
networks and, on the other, based on 'strategic actors of globaliza-

tion,' such as internationally active NGOs, experts, intellectuals, or corporations and managers. These world citizens and protagonists of globalization are successively stepping out of their national contexts and shaping the most dynamic – because most globally oriented – sectors of their societies.

Global science

The development of a global communications infrastructure is accelerating the process of broadening and intensifying transboundary research. A 'world scientific community' is in the making, one dominated by the scientists of the rich industrialized countries. The crucial factor, though, is that, by analogy to the significance of the

---

Four concepts of world cultures

1. *Mutual inclusiveness of individual cultures – the 'ecumene concept'*: The cultures that make up world society are able to learn from one another without in this way endangering their capacity for self-preservation. The interaction between cultures heightens the moments of compatibility between them. Japan's culture is generally seen as an example *par excellence* of the capacity to learn and assimilate and in this way to ensure its own self-preservation. An example pointing in the opposite direction is the emergence of Islamic and other fundamentalisms that consciously set their sights on marginalizing and excluding other cultural models (Robertson 1987).

2. *World cultures as a stock of possibilities*: There is no disputing that the world is blessed with a great diversity of cultures. This diversity, though, does not imply any closed, historically unique cultures, for instance in the sense of 'national cultural identities,' but instead owes its existence in the present to an eclectic and chance combination of cultural elements stemming from a pool of cultural options, which is, in theory, institutionalized worldwide (Moore 1966).

3. *Meta-world culture:* The dominant aspect here is – instead of the idea of a repertoire of options – the notion of a set of elements that are common to all cultures and constitute the transcultural deep structure of a meta-world culture. Hans

Küng's (1997) search for a world ethos can be seen in this context. From this perspective, he argues, the diversity of cultures rises from varieties that are based on common deep structures and emerge in the process of local sociation.

4. *The minimal world culture*: The articulation-based relations in world society are of a more or less loose nature. It is unrealistic to assume deep structures shared by all cultures, which may contribute to a universal world culture capable of growth and enlargement. Michael Walzer (1994) argues in favor of a moral minimalism immediately accessible to all humans. He cites the prophet Amos who, searching for something held unjust by all, comes up with the image of those 'that pant after the dust of the earth on the head of the poor'; this is simply unjust, and this fact is sensed by all observers, even though they may not concur with the same unanimity and certainty on what would be regarded as just treatment of the poor. In Walzer's view, the minimal culture is not the basis or point of departure of a universal world culture that could or should come about some day but merely a section of the whole – a smallest common denominator. The core of minimalism is the mutual acknowledgement of different, fully developed cultures by their protagonists – and without any call for standardization or universalization of cultures. The orientation point here is peaceful coexistence instead of a pulling down of boundaries and assimilation.

world market for the economy, the 'world scientific community' is becoming the frame of reference of science. Local, national, international, and global research is increasingly densely networked.

Dynamism, innovation, and rapid learning processes take well-networked international research centers as their point of departure. It is here that the internationally binding scientific standards are set, that the internationally leading teams of scientists conduct and publish their research, and that influential experts acquire their training and experience before becoming opinion leaders in world politics, economy, and society.

The globalization of science follows the universalistic-cosmopolitan tradition of modern science, though it also reflects the growing urgency of world problems and the increasing need for international cooperation in processing them. A number of indicators point to a trend in the direction of a globalization of science.

- Worldwide, the share of scientific publications stemming from international cooperation rose from 11.3 per cent to 20 per cent between 1980 and 1990.
- Worldwide, the number of students studying abroad increased nearly tenfold between 1950 and 1980. In the US, Germany, Italy, and France the trend continued, though at a slower pace, into the mid-1990s. The fact that hard data are very hard to come by in this area shows that the international organizations (e.g. UNESCO) are lagging behind actual developments here.
- The significance and volume of research programs and institutions associated with international organizations are on the rise. The research institutions of the World Bank, UNESCO, OECD, ILO, or CEPAL often bring together some of the world's leading experts as a means of focusing top-level international research and setting international scientific agendas. Regional integration projects are also enlarging their transboundary research programs. Other international research networks have resulted from important world conferences (e.g. the Intergovernmental Panel on Climate Change [IPCC]). Furthermore, national organizations involved in promoting research are also increasingly setting their priorities with an eye to strengthening international scientific cooperation.
- The number of major international research networks concerned with world problems is growing. The structures supporting these institutions are highly heterogeneous, as a few examples may serve to illustrate:

    - In 1957 international Antarctic research made its debut under the auspices of the United Nations. Today 25 nations, connected since 1995 via the Antarctic Managers Electronic Network, are involved in the various research projects conducted under this program.
    - The Human Genome Project, whose concerns also include the ethical, legal, and social ramifications of the project, is the world's most comprehensive research program in the field of genetic research. Established in the 1980s by the US government, it has developed into an internationally networked research venture.

- Diversitas, a global network established to investigate biodiversity, was initiated in 1991 by an international group of leading scientists; it plays an important role in the Rio follow-up process. The scientists and institutions participating in Diversitas plan international research projects, collect biodiversity research data throughout the world (e.g. via the Internet), and make these data available to the public at large (e.g. via the Internet), and work out concrete recommendations and demands for presentation to the political sphere. Diversitas is co-financed by a variety of international governmental and non-governmental organizations such as UNESCO, the International Council for Science, and the Scientific Community on Problems of the Environment.
- The International Geosphere-Biosphere Program was launched in 1986 by the International Council for Science. It funds and focuses international research projects, operates the world's most important database in this field, and offers a variety of training services.

- The transnational R&D activities of private corporations are also on the increase. At the end of the 1990s major European corporations were making between 30 and 40 per cent of their research investments outside their 'home bases.'

If it is true that, as we enter the twenty-first century, the industrialized societies are being transformed into knowledge-based economies, and the availability of knowledge (alongside the governance media law, power, and money) is the key variable involved in controlling social processes, then global science is, as it continues to network, an all-important building block in the process of forming a world society.

From international law to 'world domestic law'?

Modern societies are integrated not only via values, standards, and communication processes, but also systemically via markets, as well as on the basis of social, private, and state institutions. In the developing world society, world markets, international organizations, globally active NGOs, worldwide discourses on the universality of human rights, and the establishment of institutions designed to protect them are the germ cells that give rise to global processes of social integration. Jürgen Habermas (1992) pointed out that in complex societies normative and systematic forms of social integration are in need of legal institutionalization. The question is thus whether there are any signs that international law is evolving that could underpin the process involved in the formation of a world society (Delbrück 1998).

The paradigm of sovereignty

The international law of the first phase of the 'epoch of the nation-state,' until the middle of the nineteenth century principally customary law, is conceived as an order between nation-states based on the paradigm of state sovereignty. In this era international law consisted essentially of rules governing the intercourse between states and to a far lesser extent of value-positing norms. *Liberum ius ad bellum* was just as much a foundation of the then conception of international law as was the exclusivity of states as subjects of international law.

But in the course of the nineteenth century, modernization and industrialization processes within nation-states and the development of world markets accompanying them increasingly brought nation-states face to face with challenges that overtaxed their capacity, forcing them to seek international cooperation in a number of areas. The recognition that nation-states are highly interdependent led to a successive broadening of the paradigm of national sovereignty. It was in this way that, starting at the end of the nineteenth century, a transboundary infrastructure became necessary to foster national economic development: the Universal Postal Union, the International Telegraph Union, and the International Railway Administration may serve here to exemplify the formation of the world's first regulatory regimes.

This process, on the one hand, led to an upgrading and further specification of international law in the form of a legal codification of the new international regulative structures. On the other hand, toward the end of the nineteenth and at the beginning of the twentieth centuries, the scope of international law was – despite a number of dogmatic legal objections – widened to include the new international organizations. Strict observance of the sovereignty of nations remained the foundation of international law. At the same time, though, there is no doubt that membership of these international organizations reflected a *de facto* limitation of the sovereignty of the states concerned. The practical constraints that led to the establishment of the first international organizations mark a further step on the road to the modern international system, one in which the paradigm of the sovereign state might coexist with new forms of mutually binding agreement in the context of institutionalized international cooperation.

The ambivalent character of sovereignty in the UN charter

The establishment of the United Nations in 1945 and core elements contained in the UN Charter further relativized the sovereignty of states, thereby strengthening supranational law. By the beginning of the twentieth century international cooperation had been legally codified – above all in the fields of economics and infrastructure – and the road was now open for the international community to take on further important tasks. Peacemaking and peacekeeping as well as the advancement and enforcement of human rights became cornerstones of the UN system. The principle of state sovereignty was palpably curtailed in this process:

- The use of force by sovereign states as a means of pursuing their rights and interests, regarded for centuries as legitimate and legal (*liberum ius ad bellum*), is banned by the UN Charter (Article 2(4)).
- The Charter endows the Security Council with the authority both to keep and to enforce the peace (Chapter VII).
- The Security Council is authorized under certain conditions to intervene in the internal affairs of sovereign states to protect elementary human rights and to keep the peace (Article 2(3), UN Charter).
- The United Nations and its specialized agencies not only have the task of elaborating and codifying human rights in international conventions, they are also authorized to monitor and enforce these conventions.

So it is at this stage of the development of international law that the division of responsibilities between states and the organized community of nations is redefined. The scope of international law is widened in line with the rapidly growing number of international organizations and policy fields that were previously approached on a purely national basis, in this way coming under the purview of the international legal order. The order that emerges is an ambivalent one: on the one hand, the dominance of the principle of sovereignty is broken in some crucial points; on the other, protection of national sovereignty continues to be a core element of international law.

The emergence of elements of a world domestic law

The globalization processes presently underway are setting further alterations of international law in motion. Four phenomena are of particular significance here:

- More and more policy areas are being brought under the responsibility of international law, because national politics is no longer able to find solutions to world problems: control of weapons of mass destruction, migrant flows, protection of the world's forests and biodiversity, prosecution of human rights violations are today increasingly regarded as global issues touching the survival of mankind, issues that can no longer be left to the determination of individual states. The construct of an 'international public interest' of individual human beings and of peoples has now taken its place as a principle alongside the sovereign rights of states.
- Once NATO had intervened in Kosovo in March 1999, the war there and the circumstances accompanying it took on the character of an international conflict, laying bare some dilemmas of established international law and setting in train discussions on the further development of international law. This drew international attention to the areas of tension between two central elements of the UN Charter: the protection of human rights and the paradigm of state sovereignty. Under classical international law military action aimed at protecting and restoring human rights would have been seen as intervention in the internal affairs of a sovereign state and thus a violation of the international ban on intervention. However, a new interpretation of international law resulted from the precedence given to the protection of human rights over the principle of state sovereignty, and this can be interpreted as the result of a newly emerged international awareness of human rights. We are faced here with the need to establish an 'international regime for humanitarian intervention aimed at protecting elementary human rights' as a means of preventing vague and diffuse interpretations of international law, arbitrary intervention, and self-authorizations (as in the case of NATO's intervention in Kosovo) in the future. A

discussion is also underway on reforming the UN Security Council, which – depending on the interests of its members – can, but need not, punish human rights violations (see this volume, Chapter 5).

- NGOs are gradually developing into new subjects of international law, even though this view may not yet be shared by the dominant school of legal thought. In the framework of operational human rights protection, NGOs have the right to lodge complaints against human rights violators with international monitoring organizations; they have also increasingly gained the right to participate in consultations of international organizations and are involved in working out international conventions (e.g. the UN world conferences of the 1980s and 1990s); they have recently also been involved in compliance processes (e.g. the Desertification Convention). The fact that NGOs are being incorporated in the circle of the subjects of international law implies that the principle of international law as an order of states is being transcended.

- We are experiencing the emergence of supra-territorial regulative systems beyond the scope of international law (Teubner 1997). One good example is the development of the Internet, which is largely immune to national regulations. The actors involved in the Internet are in the process of developing a private Net-specific *lex informatica*. Similar global regulatory systems, based on the self-organization of the actors concerned and thus beyond the scope of the international law practiced by states, are emerging in other fields (Reinicke 1998). The *lex mercatoria* governing transnational economic relations between multinational corporations is an example of rules established between private actors without state involvement.

New regulatory systems for international financial markets are based on different forms of 'public/private partnership' – for instance, between privately owned banks, national central banks, and the Bank for International Settlements (BIS). These amount to a 'regulation of self-regulation.' Thus, for instance, in 1989 the G7 initiated a regime aimed at preventing international money-laundering. This has been joined by a good number of countries, and stipulates that banks must develop, and operate, control systems designed to prevent money-laundering. National banking supervisory authorities and the Financial Action Task Force (the executive organ of the regime) are responsible not for reviewing the suitability of the control instruments but for monitoring the success or failure of the measures taken. If money-laundering does not visibly decline, the banks are called on to develop further and target the instruments they are using. This idea of indirect regulation does justice to the fact that, in view of the complexity of the tasks involved, supervisory authorities are forced to rely on the cooperation and willingness of the banks to supply information. But since the banks are interested in cooperating with the supervisory authorities with a view to maintaining their reputation as serious and reliable financial institutions, this self-regulation 'in the shadow of hierarchy' (Fritz W. Scharpf) has a good chance of success. These new forms of regulation are frequently categorized as a 'third legal order,' distinguishable from national and international law.

The dominance of the nation-state as the sole source, addressee, and enforcement agency of international law has thus progressively eroded since the early phase of 'the epoch of the nation-state.' The scope of international law is widening, the paradigm of state sovereignty is giving way to a new reality of 'divided sovereignties,' more and more policy fields are based on transnational rules, the existential needs of individuals and peoples and issues of global survival are gaining weight over against the will of individual states.

Against this backdrop, Jost Delbrück sees international law as on its way to becoming 'world domestic law.' Otfried Höffe (1998), by contrast, points out that though the density of the rules governing international affairs is growing – which implies the emergence of a law shared by all nations – it is nevertheless a fact that we lack mechanisms to secure and enforce these rules. There are (in most cases) no authorized courts, often not even arbitration boards, to say nothing of any power to enforce court decisions. This is why, in the 'transition phase' in which the international legal order presently finds itself, the reality of law is left either to the goodwill of individual states or to a fortuitous and shifting balance of power. In core areas of international law that concern mankind as a whole, Höffe proposes transferring the power to interpret and enforce the law (sovereignty) to a supranational 'sanction-armed' legal order.

Habermas (1999) argues similarly, calling for a 'fully juridified cosmopolitan order' in which power is civilized by law and citizens can enjoy protection against the arbitrary rule of their own governments. The *sine qua non* for the leap from a nation-based international law to the 'cosmopolitan law of a society of citizens of the world' is, in his view, a functioning World Security Council, the binding jurisdiction of an International Criminal Court, and a widened UN General Assembly that includes not only representatives of governments but also, at a second level, a 'representation of citizens of the world.'

New lines of conflict in world society

In a networked world, structure-building processes inevitably give rise to new lines of conflict. Four important conflict constellations are emerging:

1. *Sociopolitical conflicts:* The global labor market is giving rise worldwide to fierce competition between unskilled workers. Those affected include above all the unskilled in the industrialized world; their incomes will continue to fall compared with those of better qualified workers in many OECD countries. The North is experiencing the emergence and growth of inequality. At the same time, many economies in the South as well as some societies in transformation are overburdened by the demands the world economy places on them. In Africa and Asia entire countries could become 'world welfare cases.' Whether tendencies toward global networking will prove able to help reduce worldwide tensions or lead instead to more fragmentation, conflicts, or even a new protectionism will depend on whether or not it proves possible to introduce into the global system effective mechanisms aimed at social balance. The industrialized countries will have to develop a social policy with both an internal and an external thrust – internal as a means to compensate for the distortions caused by globalization, external with a view to mitigating global conflicts.

2. *Ecology-related distributional conflicts:* The worldwide consumption of the environment continues apace. Since the environment is a limited global common, its use should be governed by global agreements which take account of the renewability of resources and set out what claims may be laid to these resources by what groups. This means that there are and will be some difficult distributional conflicts on the international agenda, as we have seen in the course of the climate talks conducted in recent years.

3. *Moral-ethical conflicts*: In many areas accelerated technological progress is raising ethical issues that need legislative action. In view of the mobility of firms and research institutions, national legislative initiatives are often doomed to founder. Discourses on

the chances and risks of gene technology, transplantation medicine, or pre-implantation diagnostics, and the search for effective regulations in these ethically sensitive fields, will therefore have to be organized along transboundary lines.

4. *One world – many world-views*. Conflict lines between winners, losers, and competitors: The end of the East/West bipolarity has lent impetus to the universalization of important social principles (human rights, democracy, market economy). Globalization, on the one hand, operates in the same direction, while, on the other, one of its effects is to generate wholly different world-views among the winners and losers as well as between the competitors caught up in the worldwide processes of change presently underway. These world-views reflect potential lines of conflict in the emerging world society:

a) People in western countries often proceed on the assumption of the 'westernization of the world,' indeed the US is fond of casting itself in the light of the 'indispensable nation' (Madeleine Albright) from which ('at the end of history') all are going to have to learn if they are to survive in the global world.

b) In Asia people have begun to speak of the 'newly decaying countries,' conjuring up in their place the 'new Pacific century,' even though this counter-project, with its thrust against western-style modernity, was somewhat dampened by the Asia crisis.

c) Benjamin Barber (1996) has drawn up yet another polarized scenario of world development, with *'jihad'* rivaling 'McWorld' for world dominance. *'Jihad'* stands for an anti-western retrogression into a new tribal consciousness based on militant fundamentalism, whereas 'McWorld' stands for global integration via the market and streamlined worlds of consumption and culture. *'Jihad'* and 'McWorld' are often influential forces in one and the same country; these are parallel trends operating in opposite directions, though both tend to destroy democratic institutions and generate a 'democracy without citizens.'

d) For a picture of a radical new bipolarism, one need only read Jean-Christophe Rufin (1993), who sees 'new lines' emerging between the civilized regions of the North and the uncivilized and violence-prone countries of the South, which are in his view in decay and no match for the challenges posed by globalism. Since, in Rufin's opinion, the South is largely insignificant economically, the North will have to use military means to protect itself against the 'barbarian world' and seek to decouple itself from the disaster potential of the South.

These divergent scenarios reflect less real developments than unrealistic 'triumphalism' on the part of the alleged winners of globalization and fears of globalization on the part of some actors who are being pushed to the margins of the world. They serve to illustrate, though, that, without any massive efforts aimed at intensifying worldwide cultural exchange and effective strategies aimed at reducing the number of losers of modernization and globalization in world society, the twenty-first century could be marked by a variety of violent conflicts, both international and domestic.

Future prospects and challenges

World society and world politics

Whether the process of forming a world society is accompanied by an increase in violent conflicts or the development of new peace zones, whether fragmentation deepens or development disparities are reduced in scope, and whether ecological crises turn into belligerent conflicts or give rise to new forms of cooperation in step with existing interdependencies – these questions depend in essence on the success or failure in restraining globalization in both institutional and legal terms.

The diagnosis presented by *Global Trends* is relatively uncontroversial. Knowledge of world problems has grown enormously in recent years. Yet many political actors continue to take their cue from action patterns from the 'epoch of the nation-state.' Global politics is still understood chiefly as an extension of national politics. The analysis conducted by *Global Trends* indicates that without new cooperation-based global governance structures globalization is apt to entail policy failure and processes of social decay. The new model calls for institutions and procedures that make it possible to work out common interests with, as Kant put it, 'cosmopolitan intent' (Habermas 1999) and a transnational approach to problem-solving.

Only in this way will it prove possible to come to terms with the new lines of conflict in world society.

Setting the stage for 'global unilateralism' or global governance?

The future of world society will depend crucially on whether the trend toward unilateralism, which has been intensifying since the 1990s, can be turned around in the new century. Samuel Huntington (1999) recently noted with concern that after 1945 the US pursued, in its own well-understood interest, a strategy of 'unilateral globalism,' which was replaced in the 1990s by a foreign policy of 'global unilateralism,' one geared to the narrow particularist interests of the superpower US. This development is weakening multilateralism, international law, and the United Nations, and impairing the confidence potential, always precarious, between North and South, and doing so in a situation in which, due to intensifying global interdependencies, it would be imperative to set the stage for new global partnerships. Political initiatives are thus needed to strengthen multilateral and supranational structures. The shape given to the EU's future foreign policy will be of great significance in this context.

One particularly difficult problem is posed by the lack of institutions suitable to enforce compliance with international agreements. The establishment of the International Criminal Court is one central project that points in the right direction. It is also becoming more and more clear that global governance must build on viable regional governance structures. On the one hand, regional integration projects are a good exercise in transboundary cooperation and compromise, the keys to governing in the multilevel system of a global governance architecture. On the other hand, regionalization works counter to any exaggerated centralization of a politics intent on building and widening global institutions, a development that must inevitably give rise to problems of legitimacy and effectiveness.

Effective and cooperative states and networks as cores of a global governance architecture

The lament bewailing the demise of the nation-state fails to recognize that nation-states will remain important actors in world society. They are the hinge between national and supranational levels of action and are important architects and fashioners of global governance architecture. Nation-states will discard their role as problem-solving agencies with all-embracing responsibility in favor of a new role as interdependence managers responsible for coordination, coherence, aggregation of interests, and long-term policy orientations. The relationship between states on the one hand and non-governmental local, national, and global actors from the economy and society on the other is likewise in the process of profound structural change: new partnerships, but also new clashes of interests (above all, between internationally mobile and less mobile actors), are taking shape. Many future problems can be solved only through joint efforts in networked structures in which governments and private actors work together in a global governance architecture. But what we often see is a lack of the institutional arrangements needed to prevent networks, with their problem-solving and action potentials, from turning into 'regulation clubs' wanting in democratic legitimation (Brock 1998). The transformation of politics in the globalization process is confronting democracy with new problems.

The dialectic of cosmopolitan mission and hegemonic world politics

The global governance discourse of the last decade has been advanced just about exclusively by the North, a fact that implies two pitfalls. First, global politics can be successful only if it proves able to involve the countries of the South, in particular giants like China, India, and Brazil, which are in the process of political reorientation. This presupposes a sharing of social burdens and an openness to the views and interests of the weaker countries of world society. Second, an exaggerated moralization of politics and an orientation of the West's open-minded globalization elites in terms of a cosmopolitan mission (worldwide enforcement of 'human rights and democracy,' the 'western model') could have disastrous unintended consequences. Humanitarian unselfishness and hegemonic power logic could add up to a new 'western interventionism' that, touting its own moral superiority, declares itself exempt from global rules. Human rights interventionism can easily be linked (intentionally or unintentionally) to the obsolete goals of hegemonic world politics. The long-term effects of the Kosovo war may move in this direction if care is not taken to develop internationally binding rules governing humanitarian intervention. Two things are needed here. On the one hand, a global governance discussion, for instance in the framework of development cooperation, that extends beyond the core countries of the western world; on the other, the discussions on humanitarian interventions and the case of Kosovo teach us that moral indignation and global missionary zeal must be restrained by means of established and universally valid procedures of conflict resolution law if we are to prevent any moral differentiation of international law and avoid any unmediated moral discrimination of alleged 'enemies.' The task here is to learn from nation-states governed by law. Crimes of violence and violations of human rights should not be judged and combated immediately with a view to moral aspects, but must instead be prosecuted within the framework of an institutionalized legal order (separation of powers).

Guiding principles for the 'epoch of globalism'

The 'epoch of globalism' will be faced with the task of working out new points of reference for politics. The following guiding principles are of central significance here:

- There is no purely national response to globalization. In view of the problems facing the world, national egoisms and solo actions are doomed to failure. They undercut the scopes of action open to politics; the only way these can be enlarged is through international cooperation.
- The coexistence of and opposition between nation-states, national interests, and exclusive claims to sovereignty constituted the core of international politics in the 'epoch of the nation-state.' The twenty-first century will see a change in this frame of reference. As it develops, world society will see nation-states assuming the role of 'provinces,' with the emerging world society as their common frame of reference.
- Cultural diversity and specific local and national milieux will grow increasingly important in the globalizing world. Nations, regions, local groups of actors, transnational communities, or corporate networks will seek their orientation in global frames of reference, though for this very reason they will also cultivate their specific cultural profiles.
- The 'epoch of the nation-state' has conceived any division of sovereignty as a zero-sum game in which one player gives up points that benefit another player. In the 'epoch of globalism' problem-solving capacities and political governance resources are *a priori* broadly dispersed. It is only through cooperation that a surplus of sovereignty can be won. Unwillingness to cooperate will, more and more, prove tantamount to political incapacitation.

The limited reach of the political culture of world society

Dense and intensive transboundary cultural dialogues are the *sine qua non* of any attempt to embed globalization in an institutional and legal framework. The political culture of world society in the twenty-first century will, however, lack some important ethical-political dimensions that constitute the basis of societal processes and identity-formation in national societies. Not even a worldwide consensus on human rights is an adequate equivalent for the civic solidarity that emerged in the national framework of western constitutional welfare states. For while specific civic solidarity can build on age-old collective identities, for which Walzer coined the term 'thick morality,' cosmopolitan identity can, at best, find support solely in the moral universalism expressed in human rights, which Walzer characterizes as 'thin morality.' There is reason to assume that 'thick morality' is the basis of active solidarity between citizens and that this solidarity also renders acceptable redistributive policies implemented within the framework of the welfare state. While the universalistic and at the same time 'thin' morality of the cosmopolitans evokes a sense of indignation about state repression and massive human rights violations, it is still unclear whether it will also suffice to support world-scale redistributive policies that would be capable of perceptibly reducing the great development disparities between nations or defusing the environment-related distributional conflicts of the future.

We may derive three conclusions from the foregoing. First, international human rights discourse must be widened to include dialogues about global (distributive) justice. Second, political initiatives can contribute significantly to preventing any erosion of 'thick morality' in the national context. Third, the EU must accept the challenge of developing successive collective identities that extend beyond the universalism of a 'thin morality,' paving the way for social integration and a balance of interests in Europe.

References

Barber, Benjamin R. (1996) *Coca-Cola und Heiliger Krieg. Wie Kapitalismus und Fundamentalismus Demokratie und Freiheit abschaffen*, Munich.

Brock, Lothar (1998) 'Die Grenzen der Demokratie: Selbstbestimmung im Kontext des globalen Strukturwandels und des sich wandelnden Verhältnisses von Staat und Markt,' *PVS-Sonderheft*, No. 29, pp. 271–91.

Burton, John (1972) *World Society*, Cambridge.

Buzan, Barry (1993) 'From International System to International Society,' *International Organization*, No. 47, pp. 327–52.

Czempiel, Ernst-Otto (1981) *Internationale Politik*, Paderborn/Munich.

Czempiel, Ernst-Otto (1993) *Weltpolitik im Umbruch*, 2nd revised edition, Munich.

Delbrück, Jost (1998) 'Von der Staatenordnung über die internationale Kooperation zur "supraterritorial or Global Governance": Wandel des zwischenstaatlichen Völkerrechts zur Rechtsordnung des Menschen und der Völker?,' in Ulrich Bartosch and Jochen Wagner (eds.) *Weltinnenpolitik*, Münster, pp. 55–66.

Falk, Richard (1995) 'Liberalism at the Global Level: The Last of the Independent Commissions?,' *Millennium: Journal of International Studies*, Vol. 24(3), pp. 563–76.

Forschungsgruppe Weltgesellschaft (1996) 'Identifizierung eines "Phantoms",' in *Politische Vierteljahresschrift*, No. 37, pp. 6–25.

Gummet, Philip (ed.) (1996) *Globalization and Public Policy*, Cheltenham.

Habermas, Jürgen (1992) *Faktizität und Geltung*, Frankfurt/M.

Habermas, Jürgen (1998) *Die postnationale Konstellation*, Frankfurt/M.

Habermas, Jürgen (1999) 'Bestialität und Humanität. Ein Krieg an den Grenzen von Recht und Moral,' *Die Zeit*, No. 18.

Höffe, Otfried (1998) 'Für und wider eine Weltrepublik,' in Christine Chwaszcza and Wolfgang Kerting (eds.) *Politische Philosophie der internationalen Beziehungen*, Frankfurt/M.

Huntington, Samuel (1999) 'Is American Hegemony Working?,' *Foreign Affairs*, March/April.

Küng, Hans (1997) *Weltethos für Weltpolitik und Weltwirtschaft*, Munich/Zurich.

Mahnkopf, Elmar and Birgit (1996) *Grenzen der Globalisierung*, Frankfurt/M.

Messner, Dirk (1997) *The Network Society*, London.

Messner, Dirk (1998) *Die Zukunft des Staates und der Politik. Möglichkeiten und Grenzen politischer Steuerung in der Weltgesellschaft*, Bonn.

Messner, Dirk and Franz Nuscheler (eds.) (1996) *Weltkonferenzen und Weltberichte*, Bonn.

Moore, Wilbert E. (1966) 'Global Sociology: The World as a Singular System,' *American Journal of Sociology*, No. 71, pp. 475–82.

Münch, Richard (1998) *Globale Dynamik, lokale Lebelswelten*, Frankfurt/M.

Paolini, Albert et al. (eds.) 1998. *Between Sovereignty and Global Governance*, New York.

Reinicke, Wolfgang (1998) *Global Public Policy*, Washington, DC.

Robertson, Roland (1987) 'Globalization and Societal Modernization. A Note on Japan and Japanese Modernization,' *Sociological Analysis*, No. 47, pp. 35–42.

Rufin, Jean-Christophe (1993) *Das Reich und die neuen Barbaren*, Berlin.

Seitz, Konrad (1998) *Der Wettlauf ins 21. Jahrhundert*, Munich.

Teubner, Gunther (ed.) (1997) *Global Law without a State*, Aldershot.

Walzer, Michael (1994) 'Moralischer Minimalismus,' *Deutsche Zeitschrift für Philosophie*, No. 1, pp. 3–13.

Young, Oran R. (ed.) 1997. *Global Governance. Drawing Insights from the Environmental Experience*, Cambridge.

Zürn, Michael (1998) *Regieren jenseits des Nationalstaates*, Frankfurt/M.

3
World Economy – Structures and Trends

Heribert Dieter

At the end of the 1990s systematic weaknesses in the world economic order were beginning to make themselves felt, notably at two levels.

On the one hand, there was the Asia crisis, which started in the middle of 1997, as well as the financial crises besetting Russia and much of Latin America. The largely unregulated international financial markets are proving to be crisis-prone and extremely cyclical. Phases marked by strong inflows of capital alternate with periods of panic-driven capital flight. In the countries affected, this leads to profound adjustment crises, both when capital flows in and when capital is rapidly withdrawn. A world economy model geared to deregulation and market-based solutions therefore appears unsuited to the twenty-first century.

On the other hand, the existing world trade order is constantly being undermined by the European Union (EU) and the United States (US). The factor responsible for this more than any other is the undiminished interest of the US and the EU in initiating large-scale regional integration projects. These projects may in the end compete with the World Trade Organization (WTO), and so undermine the unified, global trade system which has made stable economic growth possible since 1945.

While reformulating the world economy and a moderate reregulation of the international financial markets appear to be matters of

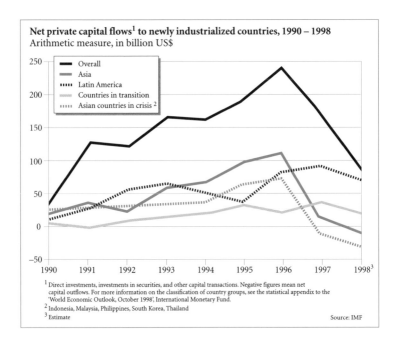

Figure 3.1

urgency, the likelihood of realizing a political project of this sort is poor. The demand for a new world economic order and the maintenance of existing multilateral institutions may find broad support in Europe, but it meets with little enthusiasm in the US.

However, the introduction of the euro may have altered this: the old-world currency, the dollar, now has a competitor. This could have an impact on the US economy in the event of an economic crisis. The end of the long, unbroken boom in the US and a downward adjustment of inflated stock prices to more realistic values could lead to a severe financial crisis in the next few years. While it is impossible to predict precisely when an adjustment will come, it is more or less certain that the current boom will not continue. It is likely that in the future the US will have to attract more international capital. Should investors no longer regard the dollar as the only world currency and increasingly switch to the euro, the US will be forced to reduce its excessive and still rising current account deficits. If the US itself was forced to face the negative impact of the existing system, this might dampen enthusiasm for the neoliberal model and lead to efforts aimed at a partial reregulation of the world financial markets.

The world economy at the outset of the twenty-first century

World economic growth slowed at the end of the 1990s. In 1998 the overall world economy grew by just under 2 per cent. For the coming decade, though, the World Bank predicts a rise in annual growth of 2.9 per cent (World Bank 1998).

The dynamics of this growth differ sharply from region to region. The average growth of the industrialized economies remains at about 2 per cent. Of the major industrialized countries, it is only the US that currently shows distinctly higher growth rates. Japan, on the other hand, which impressed the world with its above-average growth rates up to the 1990, has been unable to break out of the longest recession experienced by an industrialized country since 1945. In 1998 the Japanese economy even shrank at an accelerated rate. The economic recovery experienced in Japan since 1999 is proving to be very modest.

The development in the 1990s of the three largest industrialized economies (the US, Japan, and Germany) presented a relatively diverse picture. This is surprising in that just a few years earlier the assumption was one of uniform economic development in the centers of the world economy. The adoption of mutual economic policies by the large industrial economies that was observed in the past has thus far led to a different rates of economic growth.

In recent years Asia has experienced a marked slump in its growth dynamic. While the region generally experienced an impressive annual growth of 8.5 per cent between 1991 and 1997, with per capita economic output rising in the same period by 6.9 per cent, the Asia crisis has led to a dramatic decline. It was only the persistently high growth shown by the Chinese economy in 1998 that prevented an even more pronounced slump in the region's economic growth. Individual countries, though, were forced to accept drastic falls in their economic output: Indonesia's GDP, for instance, declined by 15.3 per cent (World Bank 1998: 194). However, and contrary to the expectations of many observers, 1999 brought visible recovery, above all in South Korea.

Declines in economic output of the kind seen in East and Southeast Asia in 1998 are a phenomenon more familiar to countries in transformation, and in particular in the states that made up the former USSR. No sustainable recovery has yet been seen in the economies of the former Soviet Union. This is especially true of Russia, whose economic output has declined further in the wake of the crisis. The sardonic comment sometimes leveled at the former USSR, describing it as an 'Upper Volta with nuclear missiles,' has become a stark reality. As early as 1997 Russia's GDP of US$404 billion had fallen to the level of the Netherlands, and in 1999 matched that of Switzerland, a country with no more than 5 per cent of Russia's population.

Table 3.1   Growth processes in the world economy, 1966–2007

1. Real gross domestic product, average annual change in per cent					
	1966–73	1974–90	1991–97	1997	1998[1]	1998–2007[2]
World	5.1	2.8	2.3	3.2	1.8	2.9
Industrialized countries	4.8	2.6	2.0	2.7	1.9	2.3
US	3.0	2.5	2.9	3.8	3.3	n.a.
Japan	9.7	3.9	1.3	0.9	–2.5	n.a.
Germany[3]	4.6	2.1	1.5	2.0	2.8	n.a.
Asia	5.5	6.3	8.5	6.4	2.4	5.7
China	9.0	9.0	11.8	9.1	7.2	n.a.
India	3.7	4.9	6.6	5.0	4.7	n.a.
Latin America	6.6	2.5	3.3	5.1	2.5	3.7
Russia	6.6	3.6	–7.1	0.9	–5.0	n.a.
Africa[4]	4.7	2.1	2.4	3.5	2.4	3.8

2. Real per capita income, average annual change in per cent					
Industrialized countries	3.9	2.0	1.3	2.2	1.4	1.9
Asia	2.9	4.3	6.9	4.9	1.0	4.3
Latin America	3.9	0.3	1.5	3.5	1.0	2.2
Russia	5.6	2.7	–7.0	1.2	–4.7	n.a.
Africa[4]	2.0	–0.9	–0.2	0.5	–0.5	1.0

1. Estimate.
2. Prognosis.
3. To 1991: without former East Germany.
4. South of the Sahara.
Source: World Bank 1998: 194–5.

The first half of 2000 showed clear indications that the Russian economy was recovering. But whether or not the Russian economy is now set to embark on a path of steady growth is difficult to say on the basis of current data. However, if no sustainable recovery is forthcoming, it must be feared that Russia, as well as other states of the former USSR – for instance, Kazakhstan – will remain cut off from the dynamics of the world economy for the foreseeable future. This has been the case for Africa for some three decades now. Its per capita economic output has been in steady decline. Five years after the end of apartheid in South Africa, it was becoming apparent that this country is likewise unable to avoid negative developments. South Africa's per capita economic output grew by only 3 per cent between 1991 and 1997, and declined by 1.6 per cent in 1998 (World Bank 1998: 195). 1999 brought no more than weak growth (roughly 2 per cent), too little in view of the economic problems facing the country – and southern Africa as a whole. The hopes that South Africa might prove to be a motor of positive economic development for at least southern Africa have thus far failed to materialize. With a few exceptions – Botswana, for instance – the African continent is caught in a downward economic spiral.

A look at the structural changes experienced by the world economy in the 1990s reveals that this period marked a turning point, though only some of the effects have been realized. Three aspects in particular are crucial to development of the world economy:

1. Toward the end of the 1990s the globalized, deregulated financial markets began to show structural vulnerability to crisis. In particular, the crises experienced by the economies of the former East Asian 'Tigers' call for the organization of financial markets and the international agencies concerned with them– above all the International Monetary Fund (IMF) – to be rethought.
2. One striking development is the rise of the European Union so that it is now a serious competitor of the US, capable of threatening its hegemony. This became evident when the euro was introduced as the official currency of the EU on January 1, 1999. For the first time since the Second World War the US dollar had a rival.
3. A further expression of the emerging rivalry between the US and the EU is to be found in the area of trade. Both are working energetically toward establishing regional integration projects. The

great powers are using free trade zones, customs unions, and other forms of trade cooperation with an eye to securing and extending their influence.

International financial markets

In the final years of the twentieth century the world economy was revealed to be unstable and crisis-prone. One striking fact here is that it is growing more and more difficult to predict economic develop- ments. One clear example is the crisis in the East Asian economies – the so-called Asia crisis. Until then, the region, which had been noted for its impressive dynamism, found itself confronted, almost overnight, by a deep economic crisis. This is less an expression of a failure of national economic policy than a reflection of the weaknesses of today's world economic order.

The crises of the late 1990s clearly showed, once again, that unreg- ulated financial markets are, at leased in certain phases, unable to fulfill the 'service function' assigned to them in the areas of production and trade. Recurrent market failures call for economic policy measures geared to limit such instabilities.

The system of fixed exchanges rates still in force in 1973 and the subsequent gradual deregulation of the world's financial markets – which, it is true, first started to take its toll in the developing world in the 1980s and 1990s – was based on the idea that financial markets are efficient and capable of processing information correctly and adequately. Today, however, we must question whether the assumption that, given sufficient information, financial markets are efficient is still tenable. Financial markets are, if we look at the empirical evidence, information-efficient only in exceptional cir- cumstances and tend to give rise to exaggerated price reactions (Filc 1998: 29).

The established world-economic order fails to take this into account. The central problem is that there is no effective global regulation of international financial transactions, even though the financial markets are far more closely integrated than commodity markets, and capital is far more mobile than other factors of production. In addition, the arrangements presently in force are not only insufficient, they are also asymmetrical in that they discipline debtors, but not creditors. National financial markets are marked by a much stricter control of the creditor side. There, in the event of bankruptcy, creditors are involved in financing the costs of debt conversion, while in the event of international debt crisis complete debt service is as a rule expected.

Institutional investors and rating agencies

In the 1990s the importance of certain globally operating actors continued to grow. These mainly included institutional investors and the big, international rating agencies; and it must be noted that instead of contributing to stabilizing the world economy these private actors were themselves one of the causes of today's problems.

Institutional investors include pension funds, insurance companies, and investment funds. In 1995 they held capital investments amounting to US$20,950 billion. Putting this figure in relation to the economic output of the major industrialized countries, we see what enormous financial capacities are in their hands: in 1994 the GDP of the G7 countries amounted to US$17,150 billion. One striking fact is how rapidly the investments of investment funds have grown in the US and Canada since 1987. The investments of such companies rose by 405 per cent (in the US) and 868 per cent (in Canada) between 1987 and 1996.

Roughly one third of the overall capital investments of institutional investors is held by pension funds (32 per cent), insurance

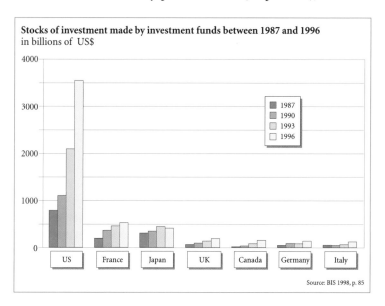

Figure 3.2

companies (39 per cent), and investment companies (29 per cent). However, differences emerge when we look at the countries of origin of these institutional investors.

Table 3.2   Investments held by institutional investors (1995)

Country of origin	Percentage of total investments held by institutional investors	Sum of investments in billions of US$
US	50	10,500
Japan	14	3,035
UK	9	1,790
France	6	1,159
Germany	5	1,113
Canada	2	493
Italy	1	223

Source: BIS 1998: 84.

In theory, a variety of actors with different goals will provide for mutually complementary behaviors and ensure the stability of both national financial markets and the global financial system. In practice, this is not the case. The regular rating of money managers' success and comparisons with the development of the overall market tend to favor 'herd behavior.' In practice, fear of a bad rating leads to risk-aversion on the part of pension and investment fund managers, especially when individual markets are suddenly regarded as critical.

True, it is not only the investment strategies of fund managers but also the interplay of institutional investors and rating agencies (private firms that rate credit risks) that are responsible for pro-cyclical behavior on the part of the financial markets. Frequently, institutional investors, and especially pensions funds, limit their investments to a given risk level. Here we see the development of the close interplay with the rating agencies. If a debtor is down-rated by a rating agency and the new rating is below the minimum standards of an institutional investor, a responsible money manager will liquidate these investments, even if he is convinced that their rating will improve over the medium term. The result is a self-reinforcing process: capital is withdrawn, which leads the rating agencies to downgrade the credit rating of debtor countries again, which in turn entails a further outflow of capital: a vicious circle.

This is clear when we look at the way that Standard & Poor's rated the Asian countries in crisis. It should be borne in mind that the Asia crisis began in 1997 and that the outflow of capital set in at that point.

Table 3.3   Development of Standard & Poor's ratings for long-term debt denominated in foreign currency

	Rating	Date
Indonesia	BBB– ↓	July 20, 1992
	BBB ↑	April 18, 1995
	BBB– ↓	October 10, 1997
	BB+ ↓	December 31, 1997
	BB ↓	January 9, 1998
	B ↓	January 27, 1998
	B– ↓	March 11, 1998
South Korea	A+ ↓	October 1, 1988
	AA– ↑	May 3, 1997
	A+ ↓	October 24, 1997
	A– ↓	November 25, 1997
	BBB– ↓	December 11, 1997
	B+ ↓	December 22, 1997
	BB+ ↑	February 28, 1998
Thailand	A– ↓	June 26, 1989
	A ↑	December 29, 1994
	A– ↓	September 3, 1997
	BBB ↓	October, 24 1997
	BBB– ↓	January 8, 1998

↓ = Downward rating; ↑ = Upward rating; ratings in italics denote appraisals with a very high risk (non-investment grade).
Source: BIS 1998: 127.

Table 3.3 makes it clear that by the time the rating agencies first began to warn of the risks in Asia any newspaper reader anywhere in the world was already aware of the financial crisis. For investments in South Korea and Indonesia the downgrading began in October

1997, several months *after* the onset of the crisis. South Korea's creditworthiness was *upgraded* in May 1997, just a few weeks prior to the outbreak of the Asia crisis. In other words, the rating agencies failed to exercise their early warning function. The downgradings undertaken in the wake of the crisis then forced institutional investors to act. In the case of investments in South Korea, for instance, fund managers of most foreign funds were forced to liquidate their investments at the latest once the rating had been reduced to 'B+,' the rating reserved for an investment with a high risk. Once the news had made the rounds of the foreign fund managers, the outflow of capital from South Korea rose dramatically, leading to short-term liquidity problems for Korean banks at the end of 1997 and the beginning of 1998 (Dieter 1998: 175).

International Monetary Fund policy

The problems caused by private actors in international financial markets might have been less severe if the International Monetary Fund's policy had not contributed to exacerbating the crises, particularly in Asia. After the outbreak of the crisis the IMF failed to stabilize the situation, and instead initiated measures that could not help but deepen an existing crisis. What it first called for was a

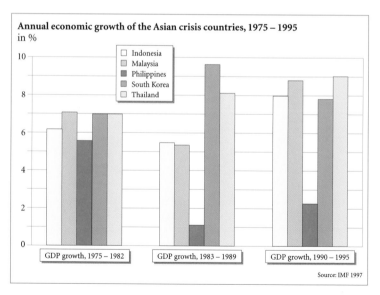

Figure 3.3

marked tightening of fiscal policy, above all reduced government spending, and a drastic increase in domestic interest rates. However, both measures proved inappropriate and counterproductive.

Starting in the mid-1970s the countries of Southeast and East Asia, which were later drawn into the crisis, had, with the exception of the Philippines, experienced an economic boom. The same economic structures that some observers, above all in the International Monetary Fund, hold responsible for the outbreak of the crisis had provided for healthy growth rates in the previous decades. This is not to say that things did not go badly wrong in the Asian countries in crisis. Nevertheless, explanations for the crisis must look at the situation prior to the crisis.

Table 3.4   Data on the macroeconomic situation of the Asian countries in crisis prior to the outbreak of the Asia crisis (1996)

	Indonesia	Malaysia	Philippines	South Korea	Thailand
Inflation rate p.a. in per cent, 1996	7.9	3.5	8.4	4.9	5.9
Deficits of public budgets in per cent of GDP, 1996	+1.4	+4.2	–0.4	/	+1.6
Current account deficit as per cent of GDP, 1996	–3.3	–4.9	–4.7	–4.9	–7.9
Savings rate as per cent of GDP, 1996	28.8	36.7	19.7	33.3	33.1

Source: IMF 1997.

The data on the economic development experienced in the later years of the crisis in Asia reveal no alarming figures for the last year before the outbreak of the crisis. Inflation rates were low, public spending budgets were in surplus or showed no more than slight deficits, and, in international terms, the savings rates were far above the rates found in other developing countries and the industrialized countries. The current account deficits might be viewed critically, though it would be wrong to interpret current account deficits on their own as an expression primarily of national economic policy and the result of decisions taken by national actors. In an age of deregulated, globalized financial markets, current account deficits also reflect the decisions of international investors who import capital into an economy. This was the case in Asia. Despite its high savings rates the region was awash with foreign capital, a factor contributing to the overheating of the economies concerned.

Bearing in mind the healthy macroeconomic situation prior to the onset of the crisis, we cannot fail to note that cuts in government spending and rising interests rates could have no other effect than to drive these economies, which were in any case shaky, into recession. It would have been more appropriate to initiate a consistent, if moderate, anti-cyclical fiscal policy while retaining current interest levels. True, the IMF did modify its policy in precisely this direction during the course of the crisis, but the move clearly came too late.

The rapid economic recovery experienced by some of the Asian countries confirms the view that the Asia crisis was mainly a liquidity crisis fueled by panic. South Korea's spectacular economic growth of 10.7 per cent in 1999 in particular that lends support to this assessment.

The crisis of the neoliberal paradigm as a consequence of the financial crises

One consequence of the Asia crisis is that the long-dominant model of globalization is now itself beset by crisis. While in the mid-1990s only a minority were criticizing the dominant neoliberal economic model, and throughout the world the ideology of deregulation and liberalization was in the ascendant, today more and more cautious and thoughtful voices are making themselves heard. For instance, observers such as Federal Reserve chief Alan Greenspan, representatives of the business sector such as BMW board member and former aid to German Chancellor Kohl, Horst Teltschik, and former German Chancellor Helmut Schmidt, are voicing their concern about market instability. Even George Soros, one of the biggest speculators of our time, has expressed concern, calling for a reregulation of the world economy. Not only did Soros publish, in 1998, a book entitled *The Crisis of Global Capitalism*, he has also continued to work toward promoting discussion on reorganization of the world economic order. At the beginning of 1999, in an article in the *Financial Times*, he proposed expanding the competence of the IMF to enable it to assume the role of a world central bank (*Financial Times*, January 4, 1999: 4).

The financial crises of recent years have spelled trouble for today's concept of globalization, understood as it is to consist of a number concepts geared to promoting the free, unregulated movement of capital, further integration of the world economy, and the continued retreat of public sector actors from the economy. Although in nearly all countries hit by crisis, whether in Asia, the Russian Federation, or Brazil, national economic policy was unpropitious and unable to prevail over the neoliberal dogma of deregulation and liberalization, it was in the end external factors that led to crisis. Only if it proves possible to prevent speculation against currencies and to restrict uncontrolled capital flows will the further integration of the world economy promote positive outcomes in the future.

Regionalism

Aside from the turbulence in the international financial markets, the second major trend to be observed in the 1990s is the growing dynamics of regionalism. Supranational cooperation went through a process of differentiation in the 1990s. The first wave of regional projects was patterned on integration based on the Western Europe model. From the very start the aim was a type of collaboration that was to go beyond dialogue and cooperation. Today, not only have the economic motives taken on a different shape, we can also distinguish three specific forms of regional collaboration: regional dialogue, regional cooperation, and regional integration in the narrower sense. These can be summed up under the general heading of regionalism or regional integration in the broader sense. But here we must also look at the term regionalization. What finds expression in regionalism is the planning will of national governments, and what we see is a process with a normative character. Regionalization refers to market-induced processes and may thus also be viewed as the sum total of regional processes. Seen in terms of the world as a whole, the outcome of numerous regional projects is the regionalization of the world economy. Regionalism is a political concept; regionalization is the actualization of this concept.

How do the three forms of regional collaboration differ? In engaging in regional dialogue the countries involved neither relinquish their sovereignty nor establish any legally binding arrangements, for instance a free trade area. Dialogue processes do not commit the participants to clearly defined goals that must be achieved jointly; they are instead based on the non-binding exchange of views, the establishment of intra-regional policy networks, and the initiation of unilateral measures. Processes of regional dialogue are especially appropriate in highly heterogeneous regions, since, as the experiences of the first wave of regional integration projects show, such regions may be especially liable to overburden a supranational project. But dialogue projects can give rise to integration processes; and if unilateral measures should prove insufficient, further-reaching arrangements, say a customs union, may hold out more promise.

Processes of cooperation and integration must be distinguished from regional dialogue. Regional integration may be defined as the gradual reduction of political and economic barriers between the nation-states involved. Integration implies that some national sovereignty is transferred to a supranational organization. Cooperation, on the other hand, is a process that forgoes the transfer of sovereignty, setting its sights instead on common interests only; in other words, it is more limited than integration.

It is difficult to distinguish precisely between integration and cooperation. When does cooperation end and integration begin? Below the level of the free trade zone, for instance, in cases in which the countries involved merely accord trade preferences to one another, it is certainly correct to speak of cooperation. But processes that aim to create free trade areas must be understood as integration processes. If the process is successful, new, further-reaching tasks will almost necessarily follow. The dynamics of the process gives rise to the need for integration, defined here as a partial renunciation of sovereignty.

The establishment of a free trade area between two sovereign nations by means of a treaty binding under international law can still be regarded as cooperation if the countries involved are not seeking to deepen the cooperation process, i.e. integration at a higher level. Even a customs union, requiring as it does agreement on common external tariffs and the establishment of an international regime to distribute customs receipts, can be seen as the beginning of an integration process. The countries involved in a customs union renounce the rights of a sovereign state to determine the conditions of transboundary trade, in this case tariffs.

Table 3.5   Regional integration of industrialized countries, newly industrialized countries (NICs), and developing countries

	Industrialized countries	NICs	Developing countries
Industrialized countries	EU, EFTA, FTAA, NAFTA, TAFTA	APEC, ASEM	FTAA, Lomé (EU-ACP)
NICs	FTAA, NAFTA, free-trade zones: EU-South Africa, EU-MERCOSUR, EU-CEFTA	AFTA	MERCOSUR
Developing countries	APEC, ASEM, FTAA	SADC, SACU	ECOWAS, LAIA, Caricom, PTA,
AFTA	ASEAN Free Trade Area		
APEC	Asia-Pacific Economic Cooperation		
ASEM	Asia-Europe Meeting		
CARICOM	Caribbean Community and Common Market		
CEFTA	Central European Free Trade Agreement		
ECOWAS	Economic Community of West African States		
EFTA	European Free Trade Association		
EU	European Union		
FTAA	Free Trade Area of the Americas		
LAIA	Latin American Integration Association		
Lomé	Agreement between the EU and associated developing countries		
MERCOSUR	Mercado Común del Cono Sur		
NAFTA	North American Free Trade Agreement		
PTA	Preferential Trade Area of Eastern and Southern		
African			
SADC	Southern African Development Community		
SACU	Southern African Customs Union		

To investigate the impact of regionalism on the world trade system, it is necessary to distinguish between two types of regionalism. On the one hand, since the end of the 1980s, initial steps have been taken toward major projects in which the world's largest economies are involved. Only the large regional projects in which at least one of the poles of the world economy is involved would be capable of having any significant impact on the world trade system.

The second type of regional integration, integration projects between smaller countries, must be viewed differently. The increase in the number of regional integration projects and other forms of regional collaboration between countries of the South constitute no threat to today's multilateral order.

Aside from the European Union, the world's large-scale projects include the Asia-Pacific Economic Cooperation (APEC), the North American Free Trade Agreement (NAFTA), and the Free Trade Area of the Americas (FTAA), which has already been decided on. A further large-scale project, the Asia Europe Meeting (ASEM), began to take shape at a meeting in March 1996 of 25 heads of government and state in Bangkok. During the second ASEM meeting, held in London in April 1998, no concrete trade-relevant resolutions were adopted. The debate on a Transatlantic Free Trade Area (TAFTA) has likewise not yet led to the signing of an agreement of this sort. There have been a number of proposals on a possible East Asian bloc in the form of a so-called East Asian Economic Caucus (EAEC), though the organization has not yet been formally constituted.

In reviewing the perspectives of the world economy and in particular the world trade order, the main points of emphasis are the dialogue processes APEC, ASEM, and TAFTA. These three projects are the most likely to undermine the existing world trade order and develop into competing projects. While these processes do not threaten to undermine the present order, that is, while they have not progressed beyond the present stage of collaboration (i.e. dialogue), a dialogue process between two of the three poles of the world economy would have the potential to develop into a closed trade system in its own right.

It should be pointed out, though, that the debate on the repercussions of regionalism is not yet over. There are two arguments here. Regionalism is seen by some as a procedure for regulating multilateralism; others see it as a challenge to multilateralism. While the latter group sees the development of regional blocs as a sign of the world economy fragmenting, the former group regards the emergence of dialogue processes between the poles of the world economy as an opportunity to develop new international regimes.

Since the end of the Cold War the three poles of the world economy have begun to establish dialogue processes. The first step was the establishment in Canberra of APEC on November 7/8, 1989, almost at the same time that the Berlin Wall came down and the end of the old, bipolar world order drew to a close. The second

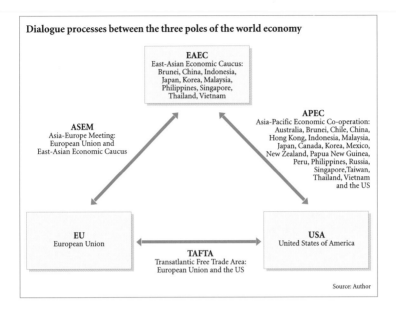

Figure 3.4

formal step was the first ASEM summit in Bangkok in March 1996. And though TAFTA has not yet been formally established, it has led to a lively debate on both sides of the Atlantic.

The status quo gives no cause for concern. Thus far none of the three dialogue processes has gone beyond the stage of a relatively noncommittal exchange of views. Still, it would be premature to rule out the emergence of a dynamic process. Since it has been in existence for over ten years, APEC offers a good starting point for analysis. We can say today that while APEC is an ambitious program, envisioning, among other things, the creation of a free trade zone and unregulated investment by the year 2020, there are as yet no signs that these ambitions are being translated into practice. It is above all unclear what forms the APEC-wide 'free trade zone' agreed on in 1994 at the APEC summit in Bogor, Indonesia, may take. Two variants are possible. A free trade zone trade could, in conformity with the WTO, be established by abolishing all trade barriers between member states. APEC would thus assume a pioneering role in the further liberalization of world trade. It is unclear how so dramatic a change of political course is to be effected in the Asian APEC countries, which have in the past tended to profit from free trade rather than actively champion it. The alternative would be for APEC to develop into a classic free trade zone offering benefits to member countries only. This would mean the emergence of an American–Asian trade bloc excluding Europe.

We can now analyze a fictitious scenario against this backdrop. What dangers would have to be anticipated if APEC, ASEM, and TAFTA were realized, if, in other words, these projects developed from dialogue projects into processes of cooperation or integration?

Any development of this kind would entail great dangers for the stability of the world economy. The present world trade regime, which already is not particularly stable, could be further weakened if the major actors were to develop competing or parallel structures of their own. One possible outcome might be that the world economy would break down into competing blocs, leading to the abandonment of today's system of a uniform trade regime.

Measures aimed at stabilizing the world economy

The 1990s was a period of far-reaching change, the effects of which are only now emerging. The challenges to the world economic order are already relatively clear. The search for options that appear politically realistic is, however, proving to be quite difficult.

Limits on balances of current accounts

Since the collapse of the Bretton Woods regime in 1973 and the start of the subsequent liberalization of the movement of capital, surpluses and deficits in the current accounts of national economies have become increasingly important. This development entailed painful adjustments for countries with current account deficits – for instance, the crisis-plagued Asian countries. Sanctions on current account surpluses, whose mirror image are deficits in the balance of capital flows, i.e. capital exports, would constitute a radical break with the present liberal regime. Against the background of the economic crises, favored as they are by powerful capital flows, it seems necessary to start thinking about measures geared to limiting current account surpluses. Actors in international financial markets have thus far regarded current account deficits as a sign of economic weakness, while surpluses have been seen as desirable, indeed often an indication of good economic performance. This, however, is a very one-sided view. For the surpluses and deficits of all economies balance each other out.

In 1944 the Bretton Woods conference was faced with two models for the architecture of the international financial system: on the one hand, the American White Plan, on which today's system is based; and on the other, the Keynes Plan, which was never realized. Keynes's – correct – idea was to impose sanctions on countries that tend persistently to achieve current account surpluses. Keynes had proposed diverting part of any possible current account surpluses to a kind of fiduciary account and, in the course of a set period of time, either annulling these funds or balancing them against current account deficits. This would have removed any incentive for national economies to contribute to increasing the volatility of the world economy by persistently aiming to achieve current account surpluses and thus capital exports.

Today's model, based on proposals formulated by Harry Dexter White, assumes that current account surpluses are automatically regulated by monetary mechanisms. The assumption is that a surplus in a country's current accounts will lead to a rise in the demand for that country's currency. This rise in demand will in turn, under a regime of flexible exchange rates, theoretically lead to a rise in the exchange rate of the domestic currency concerned, which will entail rising export prices and a reduction of the current account surplus. The problem here is that this mechanism can be hamstrung if the current account surpluses accumulated are not converted into domestic currency and instead remain abroad, to acquire assets there. Over the years Japanese actors have shown how this works. Surpluses are invested in the US, for instance in US bonds, thereby stabilizing the yen/dollar exchange rate at a low level. This has made it possible to avoid an upward revaluation of the yen, which would have entailed an adjustment of Japan's balance of current accounts.

One way of preventing high current account surpluses in the future would be to oblige central banks that achieve persistent, structural surpluses to deposit, without interest, 10 per cent of their surpluses with a new World Monetary Council. This Council would be able to assume a central function both in regulating current account balances and in stabilizing exchange rates.

As Keynes had proposed, the surpluses deposited could, after a certain period had elapsed, be transferred to the World Monetary Council and be used to improve and consolidate the Council's own capital resources and reserves. This would create an incentive for national economic policy to use appropriate measures to avoid high current account surpluses. Such proposals are not radically new. The

European Monetary Union introduced a comparable system to ensure fiscal discipline among EU member states. There, too, governments that exceed the deficit limits set by the Maastricht Treaty are required to pay a sort of penalty to the Community as a whole for their lack of fiscal discipline.

It would not be necessary to limit current account surpluses as a matter of principle. Those that are problematic are high surpluses accumulated over years, and for this reason they are the only ones that would be affected by sanction mechanisms. Looking at the data in Figure 3.5, we see that of all the large industrial countries it is presently only Japan that would be affected by sanctions for persistent surpluses. Since the beginning of the 1980s Japan has accu-

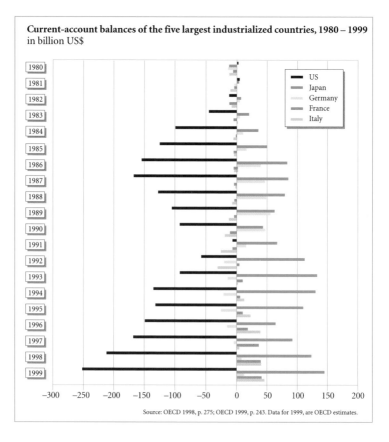

Figure 3.5

mulated high current account surpluses, US$120 billion for the years 1998 and 1999 alone, while the US has run high current account deficits since the beginning of the 1980s. With the exception of four years, its current account deficit since 1985 has been above US$100 billion. The year 1999 saw a new record deficit of US$340 billion. For the years 2000 and 2001 the OECD countries anticipate new record deficits of over US$400 billion (see OECD 1999: 243). Three European countries (Germany, France, and Italy) have, on the other hand, had no problematic developments for an even longer period of time. In the 1980s West Germany accumulated surpluses and has been forced to finance deficits since German reunification, while France and Italy accumulated surpluses in the 1990s.

One objection that might be advanced against sanctions on current account surpluses is that this would mean that the governments of nation-states would be assuming the responsibility of consumers and investors for their own decisions, though the former would have no influence on them. On closer inspection, this argument does not hold water. Despite the globalization tendencies of recent years, national economic policy continues to be at least partially able to influence decisions on investment and consumption. This is evident when we look at Japan's economic policy in the 1990s. Successive governments there have not yet succeeded in solving the problems besetting the Japanese financial sector and overcoming the economic crisis of the 1990s. What Japan attempted instead was to saddle other countries with the costs of reorganizing its financial sector. The means used to this end have included a moderately protectionist trade policy and an extremely expansive monetary policy. It is precisely the latter that has, thanks to a very low base interest rate of 0.5 per cent, contributed immensely to encouraging Japanese investors to invest abroad. Introduction of a sanction mechanism for current account surpluses would take the wind out of a monetary policy geared to capital exports.

At present this proposal has little prospect of realization, since there appear to be no political majorities for it in America, Europe, or Asia. The problems involved in realizing a concept aimed at establishing a World Monetary Council with powers to impose sanctions for current account surpluses should, however, not blind us to the fact that revising the world economic order in general and world economic relations in particular could contribute to stabilizing economic development and putting it on an even keel.

Monetary regimes

Discussions on reorganizing international monetary regimes have surfaced time and again since the 1970s. The proposals put forward by former Federal Reserve Chairman Paul Volcker are quite concrete. They are based on the idea that flexible exchange rates have contributed materially to the instabilities of the international financial and currency markets. Volcker sees exchange rate stability as conducive to both growth and competition. Businesses can make better and more efficient calculations when exchange rates are fixed or fluctuate only moderately. Volatile exchange rates, on the other hand, tend to hinder international competition. While companies can insure themselves against currency risk, such 'hedging' is expensive and works to the benefit of internationally active banks, which for this reason regularly argue against new exchange rate regimes. For example, both the Deutsche Bank and the Dresdner Bank have opposed target zones for exchange rates.

Paul Volcker has spoken out in favor of a monetary mechanism that would operate between the major industrialized countries. Modeled on the European Monetary System, such a system of target zones with defined bandwidths for exchange rate fluctuations and internationally coordinated economic policy measures would come into play when certain limit values had been reached.

Proposals made by former member of the German Bundesbank Council, Claus Köhler, aim in the same direction, i.e. fixed exchange rates in the international system. Köhler proposes fixing exchange rates with reference to purchasing power parities and securing them by means of joint interventions in currency markets. In Köhler's view, even announcing a plan of joint action would be sufficient to stabilize currency markets (Köhler 1998: 203).

The introduction of a single European currency has provided one more reason to think about a new architecture for the world monetary system. Establishing a second reserve currency alongside the US dollar should, at least theoretically, have gone some way toward facilitating the creation of a system of target zones. It is not least for this reason that Fred Bergsten, director of the American Institute for International Economics, in the spring of 1999 lent his voice to the calls for a euro/dollar exchange rate regime (Bergsten 1999).

A relatively narrow exchange rate bandwidth should be possible between the euro and the US dollar. For a period of several years now transatlantic economic relations have been marked by relatively low current account balances and comparatively parallel interest rate movements, and these would constitute favorable conditions for the stabilization of exchange rates. The European Central Bank and the US Federal Reserve, the world's two largest and most powerful central banks, could use their intervention potential to guarantee exchange rates marked by low levels of fluctuation. Once a limit value had been reached – we might think here of the ±2.25 per cent bandwidths set by the 1971 Smithsonian Agreement and the arrangement in force in the European Monetary System until 1993 – the central banks could respond with interest rate instruments and interventions in currency markets. Use of the interest rate instrument would mean that the central bank of a currency threatened with devaluation would have to raise its base rates, while in the converse case it would have to lower interest rates. Operations in currency markets could be used to directly influence supply and demand.

A transatlantic mechanism of this kind would have provided for currency markets far more predictable than they are today. The next step might be to seek to establish in East Asia first a 'currency snake' and then a monetary union, which, following a transitional phase, could be adapted to the transatlantic monetary system. It would, however, probably take at least 15–20 years to realize an East Asian monetary union.

However, it is important to bear in mind that a target zone for the exchange rate between the US dollar and the euro would not be comparable to a system of fixed exchange rates of the type in force between 1945 and 1971. For this system was based on a unilateral fixing of exchange rates. It was the German Bundesbank alone that was responsible for the stability of the Deutschmark/dollar exchange rate. The American Federal Reserve, on the other hand, guaranteed a fixed exchange rate of the US$ to an ounce of fine gold. For the Americans any form of cooperation in monetary policy would therefore be new ground. Without a major economic crisis in the US or further serious turbulence in the world economy, it seems un-realistic to expect the emergence in Washington of any political majorities for cooperation in the field of exchange rate policy.

The stumbling blocks in the way of any project of this sort are more political than economic. The reason is the incipient competi-tion between the hegemon US and a Europe that is gradually growing in importance. Even today, the Old World is, in economic terms, more significant than the US. But this development is for the most part falling on deaf ears in the US and cooperation between the European and US central banks on stabilizing exchange rates could work only if the partners were able and willing to approach this project together. Though the Europeans may be capable of taking such a step, the Americans as things stand are certainly not. This is because, on the one hand, the US is promoting extremely far-reaching economic liberalism, and on the other, the Americans have very little experience in cooperation based on partnership. Due to its unchallenged military hegemony, but also because of its still flourishing economy, the US is living in a sort of 'hegemonic illusion,' underestimating the emerging European competition, at least for the time being.

Even though any transatlantic cooperation project of this sort appears more or less unrealistic, the project nevertheless remains of interest. For it embraces the core of the transatlantic problems facing us today. Ernst-Otto Czempiel has rightly pointed out that trans-atlantic relations are poorer today than they appear to be. There are a number of reasons for this, but the main problem is lack of a non-military instrument of transatlantic cooperation (Czempiel 1999: 15). Establishing a target zone for the euro/dollar exchange rate could be an institutional pillar of renewed European–American co-operation following the end of the Cold War.

Yet it should be noted that even without a new exchange rate regime small countries can shield themselves from currency specu-lation. What is meant here in particular are limits on domestic borrowing by foreigners. Speculators must borrow in the currency targeted for devaluation if their speculation is to succeed. One possi-bility would be to limit credit to foreign borrowers. This would shorten the lever held by foreign speculators. This is, of course, not a perfect instrument. It would not restrict domestic speculation and limitations on borrowing can be evaded. But there is no doubt that as long as there are no global regulations aimed at stabilizing financial systems, national measures, with their limited scope, are justified.

The likelihood of a Tobin Tax

Discussions on a new architecture for the international financial markets have again and again led to calls for a so-called Tobin Tax. As early as 1978 James Tobin proposed a tax on all transactions involving foreign exchange as a means of throwing some 'sand' into the overly fast gears of international capital flows. It is quite likely that a Tobin Tax would hinder short-term, 'small-scale' speculation.

Monetary crises, however, such as that recently experienced in Brazil, which are accompanied by massive devaluations and tend to hit mainly NICs and countries in transformation, could probably not be effectively countered by a Tobin Tax.

Currency speculation can take at least two forms. The one is small-scale speculation that operates with small adjustments in the value of a currency with a flexible exchange rate. On the whole, this type of speculation is unlikely to lead to monetary crises, for the simple reason that a flexible course is supported, but not defended, by a central bank. But the case is different with large-scale speculation that seeks to attack a currency's fixed exchange rate. Here gains of 20–30 per cent per day are possible, and a Tobin Tax would not offer much help in this case. This poses difficulties precisely for developing countries. Large-scale speculation could be prevented only with the aid of an extremely high tax rate, and such a tax regime would bring international trade to a standstill. A tax rate of 0.1–0.25 per cent, as proposed by most proponents of a Tobin Tax, would hinder only small-scale speculation, but not the massive, large-scale speculation recently experienced in East Asia.

In general, measures aimed at impeding, or raising the cost of, international capital flows, for instance the Tobin Tax, may be elegant in theory, but are not particularly simple to translate into practice. It should be borne in mind that it is possible for the trans-actions of internationally operating actors to be shifted into free banking zones. True, capital could be taxed when it left and re-entered national financial markets, but beyond these windows transactions would remained untaxed. The proposal to make membership of the International Monetary Fund conditional on implementing a Tobin Tax would not get around the problem of free banking zones. Some very small countries might be inclined to forgo membership of the IMF in order to secure the considerable receipts that could be made by establishing an unregulated financial center. If the Tobin Tax were to be anywhere near workable, it would also be necessary to eliminate all free banking zones – an unrealistic prospect, even in international law. Finally, the creativity and criminal energy of actors in the international financial markets should not be underestimated: today we cannot even imagine what 'innovative' products the 'smart kids' in Wall Street or the City of London would devise to undermine a Tobin Tax.

The International Monetary Fund

The International Monetary Fund has for years been at the center of considerable criticism because of its economic policy recommendations. It is not least its poor performance in the crises of 1997 and 1998 that has led to calls for a fundamental reform of the IMF, calls that are wholly justified. The IMF failed in many respects in the Asia crisis. It neither predicted the crisis nor did it initiate measures to contain the crisis once it was underway. The Russian crisis of August/September 1998 likewise failed to boost confidence in the IMF's competence. On the contrary; just as in the case of the Asia crisis, the IMF failed in Russia. There the negative balance is even worse, since the IMF, from the very beginning, not only followed the transformation process in Russia and the other successor states of the Soviet Union, it was also actively involved in shaping the process. IMF advisors recommended a course of rapid liberalization and deregulation, which found its end in the crisis of the year 1998.

Reform of the IMF

Those who are against a radical reorganization of the International Monetary Fund and are interested in retaining the IMF as an institution have no choice but to plead for a modernization of the Fund. There is need for reform above all in three fields:

a) Revision of the IMF's policies: The IMF's failures in Asia prove that it is time for a reformulation of the IMF's programs. The IMF should concentrate more on the question of how to correct market failure. The answers given to this question thus far amount to prescribing more deregulation and liberalization, and this is simply not convincing. As it presently exists, the IMF is no longer able to exert any influence in stabilizing the world economy. The IMF should concentrate on providing short-term liquidity assistance not tied to conditions, though the volume of assistance provided would have to be far higher than the drawing rights presently available to IMF members. Structural reforms should no longer be an element of IMF programs, at least not in countries with intensive international linkages.

In this case even the announcement of structural reforms in the midst of economic turbulences can intensify a crisis.

b) Improvement of democratic control: It is essential to strengthen democratic control over the IMF's funds. This appears more urgent then ever, not least from the German perspective. In Germany it is the Bundesbank that provides funds to the IMF, directly and without any parliamentary control, and this procedure is no longer appropriate in today's world. Although Germany is by far the largest bilateral donor of the countries of the former Soviet Union, Germany's influence on the shape given to the IMF's policies in the former Eastern bloc has been small.

c) Separation of the IMF's financial power and the economic policy advice it provides: Both the Asia crisis and the trans-formation processes underway in the former Eastern bloc since the beginning of the 1990s prove that the IMF presents a questionable combination of financial power and policy advice on questions of economic policy. The Fund insists on fundamental changes to economic and institutional structures as a condition for the loans it grants. It should be asked whether it might not make sense to separate its lending function from its advisory function. Today the IMF's financial power smothers from the very outset any compe-tition between different approaches to economic issues.

In view of the financial crises of the 1990s it would also be worthwhile considering whether it might not make sense to region-alize the IMF. Regional funds would be able to respond more effectively to the specific problems facing a region's economies. Regional funds would be less open to the accusation that they were acting in the interest of international finance capital, neglecting the interests of a region and the people living in it. Of course, regional funds would contribute to accelerating the regionalization of the world economy, a development that might prove problematic. Abandoning a globally active IMF in favor of three or more regional funds would mean coming up with one more regional alternative for an element of a common global architecture.

Table 3.6   Assistance loans under IMF leadership in US$ billion

Country	Year	Sum of loans	IMF	World Bank	Regional developing banks	Bilateral loans
Indonesia	1997	42.3	11.2	5.5	4.5[a]	21.1
South Korea	1997	58.2	20.9	10.0	4.0[a]	23.3
Thailand	1997	17.2	4.0	1.5	1.2[a]	10.5
Sum		117.7	36.1	17.0	9.7[a]	54.9
Brazil	1998	41.5	18.0	4.5	4.5[b]	14.5
Russia	1998	22.6	15.1	6.0	–	1.5
Mexico	1995	51.6	17.8	1.5	1.3[b]	31.0

a) Asian Development Bank.
b) Interamerican Development Bank.

Source: Sachverständigenrat 1999: 18.

A new regional structure with more than one monetary fund could facilitate the resolution of crises, but only if a global structure were retained alongside the element of subsidiarity. This global body would certainly have to be something more than today's Bank for International Settlements (BIS). One option would be the World Monetary Council mentioned above; alongside the regional monetary funds, its members would include the American and European central banks. A monetary council of this kind, having both a regional and a global dimension, thanks to the inclusion in it of the US Federal Reserve Bank and the European Central Bank, would be in a position to concern itself more effectively with issues involved in the stabilization of exchange rates.

Credit relations

Reorganization of the international financial markets is one of the most important issues having a bearing on foreign and foreign trade policies. At the beginning of September 1998, for instance, former German Chancellor Helmut Schmidt called for an initiative aimed at stabilizing the world economy. He was concerned less with stabilizing exchange rates than with relations involving credit. Schmidt proposed measures geared to restraining inflows of capital and enlarging the responsibilities of banking regulatory authorities in industrialized countries (Schmidt 1998).

Possible measures will be presented here that aim at two levels. On the one hand, measures would be conceivable that seek, at the national level, to limit short-term loans. On the other hand, consideration might be given to international regulations on capital flows. This would imply further developing existing structures, especially the BIS in Basel, and establishing an entirely new organization.

Calls for improvement of the transparency of financial systems and improved banking supervision are, at first glance, plausible, though they are not necessarily in line with the experience of the 1990s. There are three factors that need to be considered:

1. So-called non-banks are not covered by improvements in banking supervision. The term 'non-banks' denotes secondary (para-monetary) financial institutions, i.e. institutional investors that are not exclusively engaged in banking activities. These include, for instance, building and loan associations or building societies, investment funds, and finance brokers. The less regulated financial systems are, the greater may be the influence of non-banks within them. Should tighter rules on banking supervision fail to cover non-banks, this would, on the one hand, constitute a competitive disadvantage for banks, while, on the other hand, it could tend to ensure that non-banks gain market shares. Improvement in banking supervision must thus also bear non-banks in mind.

2. In all of the financial crises of the 1990s loans granted by foreign banks to private borrowers from the countries concerned constituted a substantial percentage of the overall amount of credit involved. In the case of such loans, for instance those arranged between the Deutsche Bank on the one side and an Indonesian company on the other, the Indonesian banking regulatory authorities would have no possibility of intervening, even if it were an effective agency. It is not even informed of such a loan. The only supervisory authority that could intervene in this case would be the German banking authority in Berlin. This authority would of course not think of intervening in the Deutsche Bank's business policies as long as the latter posed no threat to the bank's stability. This danger was not evident in any of the crises of recent years, and so it seems unrealistic to tighten up the banking supervision rules in the donor countries.

3. An improved banking supervision system would seem incapable of preventing monetary crises. It cannot be ruled out that economic agents might modify their expectations, making risks that seem tenable today appear too risky tomorrow. The present structure of the International Monetary Fund is unable to use improved banking supervision as a means of preventing insta- bilities in international financial flows. Debts denominated in foreign currency accompanied by massive devaluations of the domestic currency will weaken any banking system, and no banking regulatory agency is in a position to change this fact.

The BIS can contribute to stabilizing the international financial system. In the past it has played a role in improving transparency and accelerating the flow of information. The 1986 Basel Accord, which provides for a minimum capital endowment of internation- ally operating banks, has heightened the transparency and stability of the international financial system.

The so-called Basel Committee on Banking Supervision has been involved in improving and unifying national banking regulatory authorities. The BIS presented its 'Core Principles for Effective Banking Supervision' at the annual joint meeting of IMF and World Bank in Hong Kong in October 1997. The BIS also presented some new approaches to improving its own statistics. These are an important source of information for those keeping an eye on individual creditors and the foreign debt of individual economies. The BIS in the future intends to report more often than it has to date, publishing quarterly reports instead of the twice-yearly reports of the past. In addition, the reports will include the highly problem- atic, so-called 'ultimate risks' (BIS 1998: 174).

There are, however, limits to any increase in the BIS's mandate. The main reason is that the BIS is the 'central bank of the central banks.' In formal terms, the BIS is a stock corporation whose shares are held by the central banks of member countries. This means that political control over the BIS's actions is limited. Up to a point, the relative autonomy of an institution of this kind is certainly useful. But democratic societies cannot forgo parliamentary control when such an institution is engaged in an eminently political role.

It is not least for this reason that we need a new regime subject to political control, an issue that is already under deliberation at the United Nations. Toward the middle of 1998 the Economic and Social Council was presented with a draft proposal on developing a 'World

Financial Organization' (WFO). The idea, devised by the Committee for Development Planning, provides for the creation of an organization with functions in the field of international capital flows that are similar to those exercised by the World Trade Organization (WTO) in the field of world trade. The basic idea is that the creation of a global market for capital was not accompanied by a parallel development of globally valid regulations or adequate security systems. A WFO could contribute to stabilizing the international financial markets by helping to establish forms of regulation of short-term capital movements which would supplement national regulations as well as by adopting guidelines for credit relations between private creditors and private debtors.

According to the Committee for Development Planning, however, the WFO would not only adopt general guidelines but also be responsible for seeing that in crises debtors and creditors were brought to one negotiating table to seek ways out of the crisis. The Committee at the same time pointed to the need for an international regime to regulate the insolvency of whole economies and create codes of conduct for internationally operating rating agencies.

According to these proposals, a WFO should also contribute to placing competition between banks from different countries on a more stable footing by standardizing national regulations. In addition, the organization would develop measures aimed at limiting short-term capital flows and supervising such capital flows.

References

Bergsten, C. Fred (1999) 'America and Europe: Clash of the Titans?,' *Foreign Affairs*, Vol. 78(2) (March/April), pp. 20–34.

BIS (Bank for International Settlements) (1998) *68th Annual Report* (April, 1 1997–March, 31 1998), Basel.

BIS (Bank for International Settlements) (2000) *70th Annual Report* (April 1, 1999–March 31, 2000), Basel.

Czempiel, Ernst-Otto (1999) 'Europa und die Atlantische Gemeinschaft,' *Aus Politik und Zeitgeschichte*, B 1–2/99, pp. 12–21.

Dieter, Heribert (1998) *Die Asienkrise: Ursachen, Konsequenzen und die Rolle des Internationalen Währungsfonds*, Marburg.

Filc, Wolfgang (1998) 'Mehr Wirtschaftswachstum durch gestaltete Finanzmärkte. Nationaler Verhaltenskodex und internationale Kooperation,' *Internationale Politik und Gesellschaft*, Vol. 1, pp. 22–38.

Huffschmid, Jörg (1998) 'Die Spielregeln der Finanzmärkte. Hintergründe der Asienkrise und Wege zu ihrer Überwindung,' *Blätter für deutsche und internationale Politik*, Vol. 8, pp. 962–73.

Huntington, Samuel P. (1999) 'The Lonely Superpower,' *Foreign Affairs*, Vol. 78(2) (March/April), pp. 35–49.

IMF (International Monetary Fund) (1997) *World Economic Outlook*, (December), Washington.

IMF (International Monetary Fund) (1998) *World Economic Outlook* (October), Washington.

Jochimsen, Reimund (1998) 'Die Europäische Wirtschafts- und Währungs-union im globalen Kontext,' paper delivered on November 12, 1998, in Rüschlikon, Switzerland.

Köhler, Claus (1998) 'Spekulation contra Entwicklungspolitik: Eine Analyse der ostasiatischen Währungskrise,' *Internationale Politik und Gesellschaft*, No. 2, pp. 191–204.

OECD (1998) *Economic Outlook* (June).

OECD (1999) *Economic Outlook* (December).

Sachverständigenrat (1999) *Jahresgutachten 1998/99*. Stuttgart.

Schmidt, Helmut (1998) 'Der globale Irrsinn. Nicht Rußland, aber das heiße Geld der Spekulanten kann eine weltweite Wirtschaftskrise auslösen,' *Die Zeit* (September 3), p. 1.

World Bank 1998: *Global Economic Indicators*, Washington.

4
World Ecology – Structures and Trends

Udo Ernst Simonis and Tanja Brühl

Environmental problems have always been part of history, life, and work. Yet the way in which environmental problems are perceived and politicized has changed. If at first it was chiefly local and regional environmental problems that were recognized, in recent years it is global environmental problems that have been a major cause of concern. Global problems can be tackled only by means of an internationally coordinated, global environmental policy; local and regional environmental policies have to be integrated into this context.

Global environmental policy has meanwhile become a highly dynamic policy field. The first UN Conference on the Human Environment (Stockholm, 1972) is generally regarded as its starting point. Since then a good number of environmental accords, both national and bilateral, though in numerous cases multilateral and global, have been signed. The efforts undertaken thus far are, however, not comprehensive enough, and they do not appear to be sufficient. So a wide policy implementation gap persists between environmental degradation and the environmental agreements that have been agreed and the compliance record that can be traced for them.

This skeptical balance is, however, not without its positive aspects. Recent years have seen the negotiation of new global environmental conventions, and already existing accords have been specified through implementation protocols. However, further efforts are needed to bring about effective regulatory instruments from the

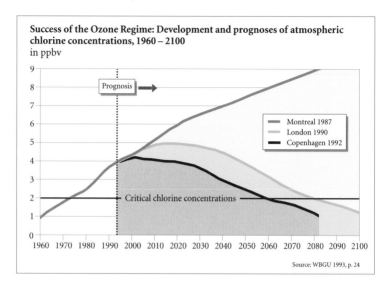

Figure 4.1

environmental agreements. Direct as well as indirect instruments should be used toward that end. Furthermore, it is essential to start restructuring environmental policy within the UN system and to look into the feasibility of establishing a new World Environment and Development Organization.

Causes of environmental degradation

In essence, three causal complexes seem to be responsible for the degradation or destruction of the environment. First, nonrenewable and renewable resources are being overused. This complex includes, *inter alia*, the exploitation of fossil fuels and the clearance of forests for firewood and to make way for agricultural and industrial uses. Second, natural sinks are being overburdened. Thus, for instance, accumulations of heavy metals in the soil and greenhouse gases in the atmosphere are reaching ever higher concentrations. Third, more and more ecosystems are being destroyed or decimated to make way for human habitat, for settlements, industrial plants, and physical infrastructure.

Prior to the industrial revolution, environmental pollution caused by human activity was generally of a *local* or *regional nature*. Today, the focus of scientific and political concern is above all *transbound-ary* or *global environmental problems*. One example is the greenhouse effect, which is leading to an increase in the average global temper-ature, with numerous though largely uncertain ecological, social, and economic consequences.

Aside from truly global environmental problems, there are also *environmental problems that occur universally*. Though local or regional in scope, these may occur anywhere in the world. Examples include growing water shortages and the degradation of soil, both of which are problems that are best handled at the local or regional level, though an international strategy seems necessary and would be helpful (German Advisory Council on Global Change 1996).

Most environmental problems are caused by *consumption* and the excessive *throughput of resources* associated with it. There is a close link between lifestyle, or level of material consumption, and envi-ronmental degradation. Someone living in an industrialized country consumes on average more goods and pollutes the environment more heavily than 30–50 people in a developing county. Global con-sumption reached a new peak in 1998, with US$24 trillion being spent, twice the figure for 1975 (UNDP 1998: 4ff.).

This consumption is, however, highly unevenly distributed. The richest 20 per cent of the world's population are responsible for some 86 per cent of all private consumer spending, while the poorest 20 per cent account for only 1.3 per cent (see Table 4.1). The disparity typical of CO_2 emissions, which go hand in hand with the distribu-tion of consumption, one of the main factors responsible for the greenhouse effect, is the following. While in the US in 1995 20.5 tons of CO_2 were emitted per capita, the equivalent figure for India was roughly 1 ton per capita. Relatively speaking, nearly one quarter (24.1 per cent) of all global CO_2 emissions originate in the US (WRI 1998: 345).

To depict consumption effects, the World Wide Fund for Nature (WWF) has developed a six-component *'consumption pressure'* indicator: grain consumption, consumption of marine fish, wood consumption, including paper, drinking water abstraction, CO_2 emissions, and cement consumption (as an expression of land con-sumption) (WWF 1998: 4). Apart from the industrialized countries, the Asian Tigers and Chile top the list here (see Figure 4.2). Consid-ering the trends, there can be no doubt that, in the future, production and consumption will have to be decoupled from resource use. This will mean making more efficient use of resources,

Table 4.1 Long-term trends in material consumption

Consumption sector	Year	World	Indus-trialized countries	Sub-saharan Africa	Arab countries	East Asia	Southeast Asia and Pacific	South Asia	Latin America and the Caribbean
Electricity in bn. of kilowatt hours	1980	6,286	5,026	147	98	390	73	161	364
	1995	12,875	9,300	255	327	1,284	278	576	772
Energy in mn of tons of oil equivalent	1975	5,575	4,338	139	67	407	102	180	306
	1994	8,504	5,611	241	287	1,019	296	457	531
Gasoline in mn of tons	1980	551	455	10	12	11	8	6	48
	1995	771	582	15	27	38	19	13	72
Cars in mn	1975	249	228	3	2	0.5	2	2	12
	1993	456	390	5	10	7	7	6	27

Source: UNDP 1998, p. 56.

an approach for which numerous examples could be cited. 'Factor Four' alone lists 50 possible ways to enhance resource effectiveness (von Weizsäcker et al. 1995). Beyond individual cases, however, it seems that not enough is being done in practice to implement this concept.

Consumption is not the only factor burdening the environment, there are also other causes of environmental degradation. *Degree of industrialization* is a highly relevant factor in this connection. The first waves of industrialization were accompanied by environmental degradation, with air, soil, and water being heavily polluted. The fear is that in the course of their industrialization the developing countries may degrade the environment in much the same way that the industrialized countries have done – unless it proves possible to decouple the use of energy and materials from the growth of gross national product (GNP).

Apart from industrialization, population growth is a further cause of environmental degradation. If overall population growth is not slowed down, it will exacerbate the consequences of industrialization. Furthermore, rapid population growth has a tendency to lead to the impoverishment of large segments of the population. Poor

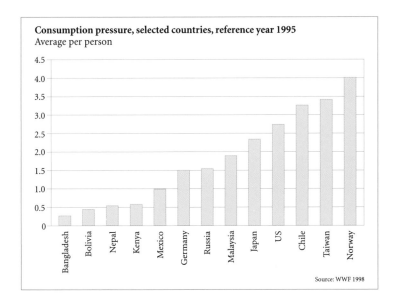

Figure 4.2

people tend to overuse natural resources such as forests and soils, poverty in this case being responsible for environmental degradation. Recent UN population projections have revised growth figures downward. Nevertheless, a doubling of the world population, with its attendant environmental problems, continues to be seen as a real possibility for the end of the century.

The need for action: strengthening global environmental governance

Though still young, environmental policy is a highly dynamic policy field. It is marked by several peculiarities. To begin with, the need for an international environmental policy had to be recognized, while other policy fields, such as security policy, have always constituted a fixed element in the list of the tasks incumbent on the state. Environmental policy is at present under strong pressure and is, therefore, caught up in an ongoing process of learning and adjustment. Pressing new ecological problems are emerging that call for regulation. There is often no clear-cut chain of cause and effect, however, and this gives rise to uncertainties for political decision-making. These may be aggravated by the close interrelationship of environmental policy with other policy fields, in particular with economic policy and international trade.

Environmental policy has its origins in the industrialized countries in the 1960s. It was here that air, soil, and water pollution first became apparent. It was clear from the beginning that pollution was diminishing people's quality of life. It was also recognized that, owing to prevailing consumption patterns and exponential economic growth, non-renewable resources (e.g. fossil fuels) would be exhausted within the foreseeable future. Thus the need for political action became self-evident. The fact that environmental degradation was recognized as a national problem was due in large measure to the work of citizens' initiatives and non-governmental organizations (NGOs). Apart from pointing to the problems, they also mobilized popular opposition to individual industrial and infrastructure projects, so contributing to awareness-building and the process of ecological sensitization.

These developments first initiated an era of *domestic environmental policy* for which efforts were largely restricted to national, or at least proximate, ecological problems. It was the US that paved the way here by establishing, in 1970, the first major national environmental authority, the Environmental Protection Agency (EPA). After the 1972 UN Conference on the Human Environment in Stockholm, other industrialized countries followed, creating ministries or agencies responsible for protecting the environment. Germany was a straggler here. Its environment ministry was not created until after the Chernobyl nuclear accident in 1986, though an initial environmental policy plan had been formulated as early as 1971, a step followed by the establishment in 1972 of an environment department in the internal affairs ministry and in 1974 by the opening of the Federal Environment Office [*Umweltbundesamt*] in Berlin.

The successful establishment of national environmental policies and institutions, however, made it increasingly clear that environmental pollution and resource degradation must also be approached at the *international level*, since, apart from its national character, the environment also has the character of an international or global common. Many environmental problems have transboundary impacts, their spread depending on geographic or climatic factors, which know no state boundaries. On the other hand, environmental problems are closely linked with the growth of the world economy and international trade, which has expanded enormously in recent decades. We need think here not only of the trade in hazardous substances, but of ecologically harmful products, techniques, and wastes as well.

Aside from growing ecological interdependencies, the complexity of physical/chemical cause-and-effect relations is a further reason for an environmental policy conceived along international lines. We are often faced with persistent effects or even irreversible environmental harm so severe that they can be dealt with, if at all, only by means of international efforts. The great number of political actors involved, with their often highly divergent interests and economic and technical capacities, are a further reason for the need for internationally coordinated action. And it is not least the close intertwining of environmental policy with other policy fields such as economic, development, and security policies that suggests internationalizing the former, especially in view of the fact that in these policy fields important decisions have long since been taken at the international level.

At the United Nations it is also generally recognized that environmental policy needs enhanced cooperation. As early as 1968 the UN General Assembly scheduled a Conference on the Human Environment, which took place in Stockholm in 1972. This first 'environmental summit' was marked by a clash of interests between North and South. Many developing countries failed to recognize environmental degradation as a problem in need of regulation. Some saw environmental protection as luxury, and insisted on their right to industrial development and economic growth. For their part, the industrialized countries were still in the initial phase of their efforts to institutionalize environmental protection and translate it into concrete programs.

There are two reasons why the Stockholm summit met, as is generally agreed, with success in spite of these conflicting interests. First, the conference laid the cornerstone of an international environmental policy. It was in particular the adoption of the plan of action and the declaration that, for many countries, constituted the basis of national environmental legislation in the years that followed. A second important result of the Stockholm summit was the establishment of the United Nations Environment Programme (UNEP) (see box on UNEP, opposite).

Twenty years later, the first environmental summit was followed by a second, important world conference, the UN Conference on Environment and Development (UNCED) in Rio de Janeiro. It was attended by delegations from more than 175 countries as well as over 1,400 NGOs. In essence, this conference was initiated through the work of and the report published by the World Commission on Environment and Development in 1987 (the so-called *Brundtland Report*). Among other things, the report injected the concept of *sustainable development* into the international discussion (see box on sustainable development, p. 107). The report made it clear that the efforts undertaken thus far by nationally oriented policy were not sufficient and called for further globalization of environmental policy.

UNCED's goal was ambitious. Proceeding from the available knowledge on the extent of global environmental degradation and worldwide social immiseration, the conference's aim was to identify approaches to sustainable development in both North and South for the coming century. However, instead taking the global and long-term view required of the main actors concerned, the negotiating stances of the participating countries were determined by short-term economic and political interests. Many industrialized countries at first dragged their heels, refusing to cooperate. At the same time their intransigence reinforced some of the developing countries in their attitude of rejection. This took the form of a willingness to

The United Nations Development Program (UNEP)

UNEP was established in the follow-up to the first UN environmental summit, held in Stockholm in 1972. UNEP is based in Nairobi, Kenya, which makes it the first UN body to have its headquarters in a developing country. UNEP is a 'program' (i.e. a secondary organ) of the UN, not a specialized agency with a specified membership and legal personality of its own. UNEP's goal is to coordinate and consolidate existing efforts in the field of environmental protection. Furthermore, UNEP has the task of developing contacts with private groups and economic actors. A further task is to provide information on the environment in order to give early warning of impending environmental threats. UNEP is funded mainly via voluntary member-state contributions, but also receives regular payments from the UN as well as additional contributions. In the 1998/99 UNEP had a budget of US$107.5 million.

Decisions on UNEP's programmatic orientation and the deployment of its funds are taken by its 58-member administrative council. This body is elected by the UN General Assembly, in accordance with a regional key, for a four-year term of office. Its one-country/one-vote principle ensures that the body has a majority from the developing countries. The decisions taken by the administrative council are carried out by the UNEP secretariat. UNEP is run by its executive director, who is elected by the General Assembly. Since April 1998 this has been Klaus Töpfer, a former German environmental minister.

Many observers regard UNEP's work as weak and unsatisfactory, and this perception has led to the advancement of a number of reform proposals from both political and academic circles. The proposals generally aim at upgrading UNEP. An initiative by Germany, Brazil, South Africa, and Singapore launched at the 18th Special Session of the General Assembly in 1997, for instance, called for the establishment in the medium term of a UN organization for global environmental issues. But since this proposal was linked neither to ongoing environmental debates nor to general efforts to reform the UN, the response it met with was lukewarm. It was suspected that this was more a publicity stunt than a serious proposal. The fact that three years later no measures had been taken to set up such an institution tends to confirm this suspicion.

But the report of the 'UN Task Force on Environment and Human Settlement,' presented in June 1998, contains concrete proposals for restructuring UNEP. Its recommendations include not only merging UNEP and HABITAT, but also closer cooperation between, or indeed the fusion of, the various convention secretariats, and intensified efforts toward coordinating international environmental policy, and these efforts would include participation of representatives of civil society.

implement environmental policies at home only if the North consented to transfer technologies and funds to the South.

Some of these demands have been met, at least nominally. Since Rio the principle of *common but differentiated responsibility* has been anchored in all multilateral environmental agreements. This means that the North has acknowledged its responsibility as the main historical source of environmental degradation. The North has at the same time conceded to the South scope for further economic growth and the right to continue to burden the environment. Structural analysis of the international treaties on the protection of the ozone layer, the Montreal Protocol, the climate, biodiversity, and the law of the seas convention has shown that the developing countries have gained new and greater bargaining power (Biermann 1998).

In spite of the – in part – sharply contrasting interests with which it has to contend, in the 1990s UNEP produced some significant results. It was instrumental in the adoption of three declarations or programs – the Rio Declaration, the Forest Declaration, and Agenda 21 – and the signing of several conventions binding under international law – in particular the Climate Convention and the Biodiversity Convention.

While the two last-named conventions are undergoing further development in the framework of regular conferences of the parties, the Commission on Sustainable Development (CSD) was placed in charge of verifying the implementation of Agenda 21 (see box on the Commission on Sustainable Development, p. 108). The CSD prepared the 19th Special UN General Assembly session dedicated to this topic, which took place in June 1997 in New York. This 'Rio + 5' Conference was to evaluate the existing and planned measures

---

Sustainable Development

Sustainable development is a normative concept which seeks to find a balance between economic efficiency, social cohesion, and ecological stability. The *Brundtland Report* chose a definition that led to intense controversy throughout the world. The task facing the world, the commission noted, is to satisfy the needs of today's generation without jeopardizing the chances of future generations to satisfy their needs.

Normative definitions inevitably take on a contentious hue when we seek to concretize them. Different interest groups may differ in the emphasis they place on the concept's components. For some, the economic component is more important than the social and ecological components, while others may tend to reverse these priorities. Put figuratively, the sides of this new 'magic triangle' differ in length in the public, social, and scientific discourse. The underlying concept, though, rests on the assumption that this triangle is an equilateral one, and that the economic, social, and ecological goals and decision processes it exemplifies are of equal import.

---

aimed at ending poverty- and civilization-related environmental degradation and reinvigorating the 'spirit of Rio'. It turned out in the end that the parties' commitment to the model of sustainable development was more of a declamatory nature, while concrete action was being determined largely by strategies of privatization and deregulation. One sign of a setback vis-à-vis the view prevalent in Rio in 1992 was that the parties were unable to agree on a final *political* declaration. While the 1997 final New York document does contain a description of the problems, confirming that the state of the environment had further deteriorated five years after Rio, no consensus was possible on the analysis of causes and on the formulation of measures designed to counter them.

Global environmental governance: aims, instruments, and institutions

The Stockholm and the Rio de Janeiro conferences are important landmarks in the emerging global environmental policy architecture.

The UN Commission on Sustainable Development (CSD)

The initiative to set up a new UN commission goes back to Agenda 21, adopted in Rio de Janeiro in 1992. The UN General Assembly took up the proposal in December 1992, establishing the Commission on Sustainable Development and placing it under the responsibility the UN Economic and Social Council (ECOSOC). The CSD has 53 members, who are elected in keeping with a regional key. It has three tasks: to monitor the implementation of Agenda 21 at the local, national, and international level; to formulate political options and guidelines for the follow-up to Rio; and to contribute to building and deepening dialogue and partnership between governments, the international community, and civil society.

The Commission's cross-cutting aims up to the year 2003 include, *inter alia*, reduction of poverty and altered patterns of consumption and production. The CSD deals annually with different priorities, for instance, with the issue of financial resources, with trade and investment, economic growth, and sustainable agriculture.

The initial hope that as a new institution dedicated to cross-cutting issues the CSD would be able to play an important role in global environmental and development policy has diminished considerably. One reason for this is that the most important environmental and development-related decisions continue to be taken in sector-oriented structures; the other is that it is for the most part only environment and development ministers are represented at CSD conferences, not, however, the ministers responsible for financial, economic, or foreign affairs.

The main means used to establish principles, standards, rules, and procedures for a given problem area are *international environmental regimes*.

The *ozone regime* can be cited as an example of a successful international environmental regime. The ozone regime regulates the production and consumption of ozone-depleting substances, particularly chlorofluorocarbons (CFCs), and is intended to check and rectify the depletion of the stratospheric ozone layer. The regime is based on the Framework Convention for the Protection of the Ozone

Layer, signed in Vienna in 1985. This convention contained no concrete reduction targets, though it defined the means by which the signatories were to cooperate in reducing, limiting, or preventing activities that deplete the ozone layer. Proceeding from this agreement on common principles and standards, the follow-up process has succeeded in specifying targets. The most important step was the signing of the 1987 Montreal Protocol, which, for the industrialized countries, provided for a 50 per cent reduction of the most common CFCs as well as a freeze on the production and consumption of halons. These goals were tightened up at the subsequent conferences of the parties to the protocol in London and Copenhagen (1990 and 1992). These conferences decided on accelerated phase-out timetables and included additional ozone-deleting substances in the reduction agreements. In accepting the setup of an instrument of financial and technology transfer (the so-called Multilateral Ozone Fund), the developing countries likewise declared their willingness to join the regime and to assume specific obligations. The outcome was an 85 per cent reduction in the worldwide consumption of CFCs by the year 1996 (compared with 1987 levels; UNEP 1998: 6). An additional reduction of CFC consumption is likely for the future, since it was only in 1996 that some newly industrializing and developing countries initiated reduction measures of their own (see Figure 4.1).

Further international regimes – modeled for the most part on the ozone regime – have been set up for other environmental media. The Framework Convention on Climate Change signed in Rio de Janeiro is likewise conceived as a framework agreement to be implemented with the help of protocols. The so-called Kyoto Protocol was the first step in this direction. This protocol, negotiated at the third conference of the parties in December 1997, for the first time sets legally binding reduction targets for six greenhouse gases (carbon dioxide, methane, nitrous oxide, CFCs, perfluorated carbons, sulfur hexfluoride). Accordingly, between 2008 and 2012 (the so-called first budget period) the industrialized countries are obliged to reduce their emissions by an average of 5.2 per cent, and the EU by 8 per cent. These targets are to be reached by increasing energy efficiency as well as by means of flexible mechanisms (see box on the Kyoto Protocol, p. 110). At the fourth conference of the parties in Buenos Aires in November of 1998 it was agreed to reach agreement by the year 2000 on the flexible mechanisms at the sixth conference of the parties in The Hague.

The Kyoto Protocol

Acclaimed by some as a decisive breakthrough in global climate policy, the Kyoto Protocol nevertheless contains some weak points, which are outlined and discussed below:

1. *Low reduction rates*: The Intergovernmental Panel on Climate Change (IPCC) noted that the world's greenhouse gas emissions must be reduced to 60 per cent of 1990 levels (this means cuts by the industrialized countries of more than 80 per cent) if the earth's climate system is to be stabilized. In view of this long-term target, the average 5.2 per cent agreed upon in the Kyoto Protocol for the industrialized countries for the years 2008–12 (first budget period) appears utterly inadequate. In anchoring binding targets, however, the protocol did take a first step in the right direction. In the future it will be necessary – by analogy with the ozone regime – to tighten reduction targets, setting a dynamic process in motion.
2. *Distinctions between the industrialized countries that many people find hard to understand*: While the EU is forced to cut its emissions by 8 per cent in the first budget period (2008–2012), the figure for Japan and the US is 7 per cent, while Australia is allowed to increase its emissions by 8 per cent, Iceland by 10 per cent, and Norway by 1 per cent. This outcome of the talks appears arbitrary to most observers.
3. Erosion of targets due to 'flexible mechanisms': The Kyoto Protocol defines as flexible mechanisms international emissions trading (ET), joint implementation (JI), the clean-development mechanism (CDM), the bubble concept, and the inclusion of sinks.

With a *trade in emissions* envisioned for the future, countries with 'few' or 'too many' emitted substances will be able to come together as trade partners, dealing in emission rights. A large part of this trade is likely to develop between the western industrialized countries, the Russian Federation, and Ukraine, since for the time being the agreement does not provide for any emission trading with the developing countries. Despite the decline in their industrial output, the Kyoto Protocol allowed Russia and Ukraine to emit as much in 2008–12 as they did in 1990. Assuming that the economic situation remains precarious in the future, this could mean trade in emission contingents that exist only on paper (so-called 'hot air'). This would not help the global climate system. In general, however, the crucial advantage of emission trading is quite evident: the instrument can be adjusted with a view to the ecological situation and is highly advantageous in economic and efficiency terms. As for other, flexible instruments, the industrialized countries are allowed to meet part of their reduction obligations by carrying out projects in other countries. If such projects are conducted in other industrialized countries or countries in transition (so-called Annex I countries), the Kyoto Protocol speaks of joint implementation. The clean-development mechanism (CDM) was introduced into the protocol to cover such projects carried out between industrialized and developing countries. The underlying idea is that a given country's industrial and energy-producing facilities may be converted with the help of funds and technologies from another country in such a way as to reduce greenhouse gases. The cuts achieved in this way are to be credited wholly or in part to the account of the donor country (so-called crediting), although the relevant permissible percentages are still a matter of dispute. One good reason for a joint effort of this sort is that it makes more sense to achieve internationally higher emission cuts for one and the same amount of money (and investment funds) than would be possible at the national level. To avoid 'ransoming practices', such measures may, however, have to be limited to certain levels (caps or ceilings). In this way the greater part of the reduction measures might have to be carried out in the industrialized countries themselves.

While it was above all US arguments that led to the inclusion of the flexible mechanisms in the Kyoto Protocol, it was mainly due to EU insistence that the *bubble concept* was adopted. It concedes to individual countries the right to join forces with others to form a 'bubble', in this way jointly meeting the reduction targets set out under the protocol. While the EU's argument was that as a regional organization it was automatically entitled to form a 'bubble,' other countries are now also allowed to join forces to form such bubbles.

Inclusion of sinks: Sinks are the places in which CO_2 is stored or sequestered, e.g. in forests, certain soils, and the oceans. The Kyoto Protocol provides for making allowance for sinks in the process of verifying compliance with the national reduction targets. In this way, aside from technical reductions of emissions in industry, commerce, and transportation, the capacity of natural sinks to absorb greenhouse gases has also been given relevance in climate policy. Accordingly, the dispute over what should be recognized as a sink, and to what extent it may be credited, is vehement. Since such decisions are definitely in need of consensus, the IPCC was asked to clarify the issue, and the decision on this instrument has been put off until the next conference of the parties.

The year 1992 also saw the adoption of the Biodiversity Convention, which is designed to protect biological diversity (protection aspect) and regulate its sustainable use (use aspect). The Desertification Convention, adopted in 1994 and in force since 1996, is designed to combat soil degradation in arid regions experiencing serious drought and desertification. This – regionally limited – convention could, in the medium to long term, give rise to a global convention on the protection of soils. There are also many other international environmental regimes, such as those on the protection of the oceans, individual rivers or lakes, or specific animal and plant species (see box on Important Environmental Agreements).

A look at the 'degree of maturity' of the various regimes may serve to highlight the dynamics of international environmental policy. Alongside solidly established and successful regimes like the ozone regime, there are rather weak international regimes like the PIC Convention (Prior Informed Consent) signed in September 1998. This convention is designed to protect man and the environment against the inappropriate use of pesticides and other chemicals by enabling the developing countries to decide in the future whether or not to agree on importing hazardous substances.

The POP Regime, designed to reduce persistent organic pollutants, so-called POPs, which include DDT and accumulate in animal and

Important International Environmental Agreements

(Selected treaties with the years in which they were signed, and came into force)

- Convention for the International Regulation of Whaling (1946, in force 1948)
- International Convention on the Prevention of Pollution of the Sea by Oil (OILPOL, 1954, in force 1958)
- Convention on Fishing and the Conservation of Living Resources of the High Seas (1958, in force 1966)
- Convention on Wetlands of International Importance, especially as Waterfowl Habitat (Ramsar Convention, 1971, in force 1975)
- Convention on International Trade in Endangered Species of Wild Fauna and Flora (CITES, 1973, in force 1975)
- International Convention for the Prevention of Pollution from Ships (MARPOL, 1973, in force 1983)
- International Convention for the Protection of the Ozone Layer (1985, in force 1998); Montreal Protocol (1987, in force 1989)
- International Convention on the Control of Transboundary Movements of Hazardous Wastes and their Disposal (Basel Convention, 1989, in force 1992)
- United Nations Convention on Biological Diversity (1992, in force 1993)
- United Nations Framework Convention on Climate Change (1992, in force 1994); Kyoto Protocol (1997, not yet in force)
- United Nations Convention to Combat Desertification in Countries Experiencing Serious Drought and/or Desertification, particularly in Africa (1994, in force 1996)
- Global Convention on the International Trade in Hazardous Substances (PIC Convention 1998, not yet in force)

human body tissues, is still in the negotiation phase. In June 1998 a commission was empaneled to negotiate an international convention by the year 2000.

The creation of international environmental regimes to regulate individual environmental problems is, in general terms, an adequate approach to dealing with such problems, though international regimes also have their weak points, particularly since they often lack provisions on dealing with non-complying countries. Furthermore, an approach geared to specific media or sectors can divert attention from existing interdependencies. If each and every international regime builds up its own institutional apparatus (with secretariat, conference of the parties, advisory boards), this could lead to fragmentation and discrimination against the developing countries. Thanks to their low capacity as regards funding and manpower, these countries are often not able to participate in the conferences nor are they in a position to provide sufficient support and funding to implement the signed environmental regimes.

Local Agenda 21

Agenda 21, adopted in Rio de Janeiro, underlines in Chapter 28 the role of municipalities in implementing sustainable development. Municipalities have an important role to play in setting up, administering, and maintaining economic, social, and environmental infrastructure, contributing in this way not only to municipal but also to national and international environmental policy. Agenda 21 therefore calls on the world's municipal administrations to enter into a dialogue with their citizens, public organizations, and the private sector at large as well as to adopt their own local Agenda 21 (LA 21).

By the end of 1996, more than 1,800 municipalities in 64 countries had embarked on such LA 21 processes, most of them, though, in industrial countries. In the meantime their number has grown considerably. Generally, participation of municipalities is greatest in the countries where there are national platforms on Agenda 21 or other coordinating institutions.

In Germany, for instance, in the year 2000 more than 1,200 municipalities were involved in the Agenda 21. In view of Germany's total of 16,000 municipalities, though, this may not seem much. In Italy some 30 per cent of all municipalities are participating in the Agenda 21 process, in the UK the figure is nearly 60 per cent, and in Norway 99 per cent of local communities are involved.

Aside from the diversity and number of the actors involved, the issue of interlinking the individual policy levels in environmental policy is increasingly proving to be sensitive. International resolutions are signed by governments, though they can take effect only when they have adopted and implemented at the local and regional level. The Local Agenda 21 movement, with its goal of implementing sustainable development at the municipal level, is symbolic of this (see box on Local Agenda 21). This movement shows that it is only through a coordinated effort involving all the different levels of politics – from the local to the national, up to the global level – that an effective environmental policy can be developed and implemented.

Innovations in global environmental governance

New actors

If environmental policy was, in its infancy, understood basically as domestic environmental policy, only later taking on the role of external environmental policy – the state being in both cases the central actor – we can now speak without reservation of *global environmental policy*. This, however, does not imply that the day of the state as the primary actor of politics is over or that the state should or could be released from its responsibility in this regard. What is meant is that states may be overtaxed as actors when endowed with exclusive responsibility, and it is exactly for this reason that new actors are entering the stage.

Thus, for instance, the 100+ cities responsible for some 10 per cent of global CO_2 emissions have joined forces to forge a 'climate alliance.' To reduce their own CO_2 emissions, these communities are stepping up their investments in local and regional public transportation, in solar technology, and in large-scale public awareness campaigns. Using methods of this sort, Toronto has managed to cut its CO_2 emissions by 20 per cent (Flavin 1998: 17). Individual companies and branches of industry have announced voluntary commitments in this regard. German industry, for instance, on the occasion of the first conference of the parties to the Climate Convention, announced its intention to cut its CO_2 emissions by 25 per cent as compared with the year 1990. States, too, have made pledges. The declared goal of the German government is to cut CO_2

by 25 per cent by the year 2005, and a specific program was recently launched.

Alongside cities, municipalities, and industry, NGOs are active in environmental policy, including large international NGOs such as Greenpeace, WWF, and Friends of the Earth. The increasingly close interaction between states and NGOs may be regarded as a special characteristic of global environmental policy.

This interaction becomes particularly clear when we consider the role of NGOs at environmental conferences. At the first UN environmental conference in Stockholm in 1972 only 255 NGOs were accredited as official participants; at the second conference in Rio de Janeiro in 1992 there were over five times as many NGOs officially represented. While the first NGOs to be accredited were internationally active ones, since 1996 national and local NGOs have been officially welcome as well (see Table 4.2).

Table 4.2   Accreditation of NGOs to Environmental Conferences

Year	Environmental conference	No. of accredited NGOs
1972	UNCHE Stockholm	255
1992	UNCED Rio	1,420
1994	Biodiversity Convention: 1st conference of the parties	106
1995	Climate Convention: 1st conference of the parties	177
1996	Climate Convention: 1st conference of the parties	212
1996	Biodiversity Convention: 1st conference of the parties	264

Sources: Feraru 1974: 33; Morphet 1996: 124ff.; Yamin 1997: 8f.

The involvement of NGOs influences the course and the outcome of conference diplomacy. While 'green' NGOs, offshoots of the environmental movement, are generally concerned to tighten up political regulations with a view to protecting the environment (the environmental 'activists'), industry-oriented 'gray' NGOs are for the most part to be found on the side of the environmental 'heel-draggers.' Existing alliances of states are in this way influenced in one direction or another by accredited NGOs. The climate negotiations, for instance, saw the emergence of a special alliance consisting of environmental NGOs, the small island countries potentially affected by the greenhouse effect (the Association of Small Island States – AOSIS), and – in issues concerning details – member countries of the EU. On the other hand, the oil-exporting countries (OPEC) have often enjoyed the support of NGOs set up by the oil industry. This shows that while on the one hand new alliances can be built to support an effective environmental policy, the involvement of NGOs can on the other hand also strengthen the hand of the 'eternal nay-sayers.'

The assessment of the increased admission of NGOs to official negotiations tend to differ. While some observers see this as an act of democratization of international negotiations, others question the legitimation of NGOs, since they may not be elected and may not be obliged to account for or justify their activities. But it is a fact that NGOs offer a variety of services such as inexpensive research, policy advice, and public awareness-building and contribute to toward monitoring the commitments of signatory states. It is not only in the negotiations at world summits and parallel events ('counter-summits') that NGOs are active, at the local and regional level they may also be important partners in initiating and implementing environmental policy.

New instruments

One institutional innovation that has been gaining ground in connection with the globalization of environmental policy since the mid-1980s is the enlargement of the set of instruments used for direct control. Financial and technology transfers provide the developing countries with incentives to assume and meet international obligations. New mechanisms of financial and technology transfer have been anchored in nearly all international environmental regimes. In 1990, for instance, the Multilateral Ozone Fund was set up within the framework of the Montreal Protocol. The fund, which is supported on a voluntary basis by the industrialized countries, is used to finance the setup of CFC-free plants and technologies in developing countries (so-called conversion). Another important instrument is the Global Environment Facility (GEF), which is used to finance projects under different environmental regimes (see box on the Global Environment Facility, p. 119).

There are other far-reaching examples of financial and technology transfers: For instance, Article 1 of the Biodiversity Convention sets out a triad consisting of conservation of biological diversity, sustainable utilization of its elements, and a balanced and equitable distribution of the benefits accruing from the use of genetic resources. As guiding principles, this article provides for an adequate access to genetic resources, an adequate transfer of relevant technologies, and adequate funding. The provisions of the Climate Convention are similar and the Kyoto Protocol provides for the Clean Development Mechanism.

Aside from such direct instruments, means of indirect control can also be used to improve global environmental policy. The concern here is chiefly capacity-building: training of personnel, strengthening of national administrations, funding of relevant research, development of information and communication, establishing clearing-house functions. While capacity-building in general is conceived as the task of all countries, the primary concern here is the developing world.

New decision-making and negotiating procedures

A further innovation can be seen in the manner in which decisions are prepared and taken. Recently, at the international level, a new, double-weighted voting procedure has come into being (see Multilateral Ozone Fund and GEF). While the general UN principle is 'one-country/one-vote' (which gives the developing countries a

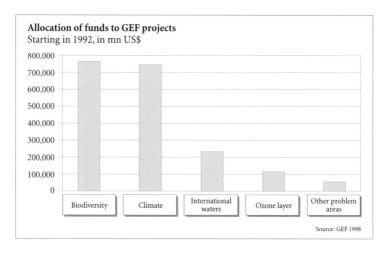

Figure 4.3

The Global Environment Facility (GEF)

The GEF is a financial mechanism that provides funds for environmental protection projects for developing countries and countries in transition. The projects promoted thus far have been in four areas: climate protection, protection of biodiversity and of international waters, and protection of the ozone layer. The GEF was set up in 1991 as a three-year pilot project on the initiative of France and Germany. The main aim was to meet the need for financing mechanisms for international environmental protection that was addressed in the 1987 Brundtland Report.

In March 1994 the GEF was reformed, on the one hand in order to improve its information functions, on the other to give a more democratic shape to its voting procedures. In the first, pilot phase decisions on allocations of project funds were still taken by the World Bank, in which only the states that pay contributions have voting rights, today the decisions are taken by the GEF Council, which consists of 32 members; 16 of them are from developing countries, 14 from OECD countries, and two from countries in transition. Both the group of industrialized countries and the group of developing countries are able to block decisions, which means that it is necessary to seek consensus.

The GEF's financial framework is over US$2 billion for a three-year period.

---

majority of votes), the rule governing the Bretton Woods institutions (World Bank, IMF) is that a member country has voting rights in accordance with the financial shares it holds (this 'one-dollar/one-vote' principle gives the industrialized countries the majority). In global environmental policy these two procedures have been linked in the sensitive area of financial transfers. Both in the Multilateral Ozone Fund and in the GEF decisions are taken in accordance with a coupled procedure. In the GEF decisions require a two-thirds majority, and this majority must represent both 60 per cent of the countries involved in the Global Environment Facility (GEF) and 60 per cent of financial contributions to the GEF. This procedure amounts in effect to North/South parity, one that accords to both developing countries and industrialized countries an effective veto position (Biermann and Simonis 1998: 8).

The increasing use of such voting procedures has led to changes in the forms of negotiation. More and more frequently, technical, economic, and political issues are negotiated separately, which means setting up several working groups or committees. Consequently, the new environmental regimes contain, beside the conferences of the parties, usually one committee each for technical questions and implementation issues. This differentiation of the communication process (and 'depoliticization' of technical questions) has, though, occasionally gone wrong. For instance, the subcommittee on scientific and technical questions of the biodiversity regime (the Subsidiary Body on Technical and Technological Advice, SBSTTA) has developed into a 'mini-conference of the parties,' where political issues are discussed controversially.

Legal enforcement mechanisms

The number of multilateral environmental agreements has increased enormously since the 1960s. And yet the degradation of the environment continues apace. One way of countering this development is to tighten up the rules and regulations, for instance, by adopting additional protocols to existing conventions. Another possibility is to improve compliance with given rules, which would mean sharpening the legal enforcement instruments. This could include both incentives and sanctions.

At present only a few international environmental regimes feature a specific enforcement mechanism, and those that do have such a mechanism are for the most part of a cooperative nature. What this means is that the signatories are bound to undertake joint efforts to support a non-complying state in such a way as to enable it to meet its obligations.

This type of enforcement was first practiced in the ozone regime. The Montreal Protocol provides for a reporting system which requires all signatories to disclose, within a set period, both the technical details and the measures they have undertaken to comply with the protocol. A special committee set up for this purpose, the so-called Implementation Committee, verifies the reports and may recommend to the Conference of the Parties further measures that ought to be taken. In the past years the Committee has been concerned both with non-compliance and with cases of (unintended) self-incrimination on the part of some countries in transition. The Committee's approach has been cooperative in such cases. The countries concerned have been questioned on the reasons for their non-compliance, and a joint search for a way to ensure future compliance has been initiated. These supportive measures (which may include financial and technology transfers) do not rule out the imposition of sanctions. Beside formal admonitions, such sanctions may extend to cancellation of benefits already approved. All these measures have been fixed in an (albeit legally non-binding) list kept by the Committee.

The climate regime, i.e. both the Framework Convention and the Kyoto Protocol, is also set to be equipped with enforcement mechanisms. The member states of the EU in particular are calling for a swift formulation of such arrangements. They are demanding a new body with the power to impose sanctions in cases of non-compliance with the regulations agreed on.

Both the Basel Convention on the Control of Transboundary Movements of Hazardous Wastes and the Convention on the Northeast Atlantic include legal enforcement mechanisms. Discussion is underway on the introduction of such mechanisms for other environmental regimes, such as the Desertification Convention.

Future political options

Global environmental policy is, as was noted, a dynamic policy field. In less than 30 years citizens have been encouraged to develop a environmental awareness, success has been met with at the government level in creating a domestic environmental policy, and at the international level important building blocks of a global environmental policy (ozone, climate, biodiversity, desertification, oceans) have been put in place. Despite these successes, the efforts undertaken thus far are not sufficient, and the environment continues to be degraded and destroyed. The tasks for the future will consequently include consolidation and expansion of the existing instruments, creation of new and strengthening of existing institutions, and, in particular, improved coordination of the interactions between the different levels of policy.

Consolidating and expanding existing instruments

The core element of global environmental policy consists of the international regimes aimed at regulating a given environmental medium. Rules of behavior have now been established for nearly all globally relevant areas, except soil and water. But not all countries are in compliance with the rules, nor does this non-compliance always lead to imposition of the respective sanctions. It is therefore essential that in the future additional and effective enforcement mechanisms be built into the international regimes. This would include in particular a catalogue of sanctions for cases of non-compliance, and these sanctions should be monitored continuously. Aside from supportive ('rewarding') mechanisms, this catalogue should also include 'punitive' sanctions.

Creating new institutions

Strengthening UNEP and streamlining CSD could give global environmental policy new clout, though this minimalist strategy is certainly not a certain solution to the problem. Instead of merely calling for increased efficiency and improved coordination, the time has come to look into a proposal that has been advanced for a World Organization for Environment and Development as a new UN special agency (Biermann and Simonis 1998). This new institution

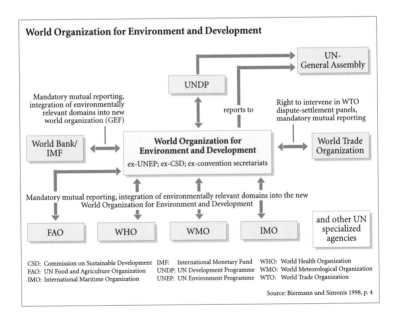

Figure 4.4

should, as a minimum, integrate UNEP, the CSD, and the relevant environmental convention secretariats. UNDP, with its huge project budget, could also be integrated into it. Care would have to be taken to ensure that the new organization would collaborate with the Bretton Woods institutions, the WTO, and the other environmentally relevant UN organizations (see Figure 4.4).

Coordinating the interactions between the various actors

Environmental policy can be effective only if the actors involved at the different levels (local, national, regional, global) cooperate more closely. There is still a lot of work to be done here. The 'higher' levels should, for instance, define the framework and at the same time respond dynamically to initiatives from the 'lower' (local or national) levels. Environmental policy is also strongly intertwined with other policy fields, it is a cross-sectional issue. This is why more coordination is called for, an effect that could be achieved by intermeshing institutions responsible for environmental and trade policy.

References

Benedick, Richard E. (1998) *Ozone Diplomacy. New Directions in Safeguarding the Planet,* Cambridge, MA.

Biermann, Frank (1998) *Weltumwletpolitik zwischen Nord und Süd,* Baden-Baden.

Biermann, Frank and Simonis, Udo Ernst (1998) *A World Environment and Development Organization. Functions, Opportunities, Issues,* Policy Paper 9, Development and Peace Foundation, Bonn.

Feraru, Anne Thompson (1974) 'Transnational Political Interests and the Global Environment,' *International Organization,* Vol. 28(1) (Winter), pp. 31–60.

Flavin, Christopher (1998) 'Last Tango in Buenos Aires,' *World Watch* (November/December), pp. 10–18.

GEF (Global Environment Facility) (1998) <http://www.gefweb.org/operport/PROGLIST.PDF>.

German Advisory Council on Global Change (1996) *World in Transition. Ways towards Global Environmental Solutions, Annual Report 1995,* Berlin, Heidelberg, and New York.

German-American Academic Council (1999) *Climate Change Policy in Germany and the United States.* Conference Proceedings, Bonn and Washington, DC.

Gettkant, Andreas, Simonis, Udo. E., and Suplie, Jessica (1997) *Biopolicy for the Future. Co-operation or Conflict between North and South,* Policy Paper 4, Development and Peace Foundation, Bonn.

Jänicke, Martin and Weidner, Helmut (eds.) (1995) *Successful Environmental Policy. A Critical Evaluation of 24 Cases.* Berlin.

Morphet, Sally (1996) 'NGOs and the Environment,' in P. Willetts (ed.) *'The Conscience of the World'. The Influence of Non-Governmental Organizations in the UN System*, London, pp. 116–46.

Simonis, Udo E. (1998) 'Internationally Tradeable Emission Certificates. Efficiency and Equity in Linking Environmental Protection with Economic Development,' in H. J. Schellnhuber and V. Wenzel (eds.) *Earth System Analysis. Integrating Science for Sustainability*, Berlin, Heidelberg, and New York, pp. 321–36.

UNDP (United Nations Development Programme) (1998) *Human Development Report 1998*, New York and Oxford.

UNEP (United Nations Environment Programme) (1998) *Report of the Secretariat on Information Provided by the Parties in Accordance with Article 7 and 9 of the Montreal Protocol, Tenth Meeting of the Parties to the Montreal Protocol on Substances that Deplete the Ozone Layer* [UNEP, OzL.Pro.10/3], Cairo.

WBGU (Wissenschaftlicher Beirat der Bundesregierung) (1998) *Welt im Wandel*, Berlin u.a.

Weizsäcker, Ernst Elrich von, Amory B. Lovins, and L. Hunter Lovins (1997) *Factor Four: Doubling Wealth, Halving Resource Use*, London.

World Commission on Environment and Development (1987) *Our Common Future* (Brundtland Report), Oxford and New York.

World Resources Institute (1998) *World Resources 1998–1999*, New York and Oxford.

World Wide Fund for Nature (1998) *Living Planet Report: Overconsumption is driving the rapid decline of the world's natural environment*, Gland. <http://www.panda.org/livingplanet/home.html>.

Yamin, Farhana (1997) *NGO Participation in the Convention on Biological Diversity, Foundation of International Environmental Law and Development* Working Paper, London.

Young, Oran, R. (1989) *International Cooperation. Building Regimes for Natural Resources and the Environment*, Ithaca, NY.

5
World Politics – Structures and Trends

Dirk Messner and Franz Nuscheler

The last decade of the twentieth century was ushered in by an event of world-historical import: the end of East–West conflict, marked as it was by sharp antagonisms and the arms race. When the bipolar, macro-constellation character of this conflict collapsed, the talk was not of 'world politics in the process of change' or a 'new world politics,' but of a 'new world order.' At that point, Immanuel Kant's vision of 'perpetual peace' seemed almost within reach, especially in view of the fact that the peaceful revolutions in Eastern Europe were accompanied by a 'third wave of democratization' elsewhere in the world.

The end of the Cold War also engendered hopes that the United Nations might finally be able to meet the tasks and aims set out in its Charter, above all peacekeeping and the protection of human rights. 1989/90, the years of world-political change, were filled with great hope, visions – and illusions. There was much talk of a *neue Unübersichtlichkeit*, a 'new intransparency.' Dieter Senghaas (1994) summed up the uncertainties surrounding global trends following the 'decomposition of a macrostructure' in the oracular question: 'Where is the world headed?' The war in Kosovo added topicality and urgency to the question, casting the nascent hopes for peace at the beginning of the new decade in a more sober light.

At the beginning of the new century a 'unipolar world order' seems to have risen from the ruins of the bipolar world order. This,

Figure 5.1

however, is not a stable order for it incites anti-hegemonic resistance and is incapable of solving existing global problems. The dawning 'age of globalism' will see, over time and in opposition to patterns of international behavior and action, the emergence of new forms of international cooperation and national decision-making that may be termed global governance. This is an attempt to find regulative solutions to the effects of globalization and the problems of interdependence. The core thesis is that global governance is a necessary response to the challenges of global trends.

New turbulences and anarchic tendencies

The fact that the end of East–West conflict revealed the underlying contours of the international system's polycentric structure is not the only reason why world politics has become more opaque. While this polycentrism was always present, manifesting itself in the Nonaligned Movement, in the rise of new regional powers, and the emergence of new world-economic power centers (the EU, Asia/Pacific), it was nevertheless masked by the bipolar macrostructure of the East–West conflict. The collapse of the Soviet Union and the socialist bloc that it dominated, the emergence of a new, unstable polity, and the uncertainties that surround the future development Russia as an economically weakened and politically unstable nuclear power have added to the 'new intransparency.'

World politics has also become more turbulent and conflict-ridden. Following the end of the 'great security dilemma' which, from the end of the Second World War, held world politics in a tense though relatively stable state of 'organized peacelessness,' the number of wars has declined, although the same period has also experienced civil wars, even in Europe. The re-emergence of ethnic nationalism, which has become an explosive factor in multi-ethnic polities, and the emergence of numerous ethno-political conflicts have prompted analysts of longer-term world-political development trends to see something of the order of a return to 'yesteryear.'

In some regions of the world – in the Balkans, in the Caucasus, in Afghanistan, or in Indonesia – we have also witnessed tendencies that are moving in the direction of chaotic disintegration. The degeneration of political culture and the brutalization of social conflicts recall more the Hobbesian state of nature, the 'war of all against all,' than Kant's vision of perpetual peace. Many catastrophe theorists have conjured up world-political horror scenarios, one discerning burgeoning spheres of anarchy (Kaplan 1996), another discovering a 'pandemonium' consisting of polities whose existence is little more than virtual (Moynihan 1993), a third seeing an impending division of the world into spheres of civilization and of barbarism (Rufin 1996). The April 1999 issue of *Le Monde Diplomatique* saw the birth of a new group of countries: *Entités chaotiques ingouvernables*. The war in Kosovo has provided graphic new evidence in support of apocalyptic visions of this kind. The term genocide has been used more often in the current period than it has in past decades.

Such Hobbesian interpretations and exaggerated views of global trends are wholly blind to counter-development trends. The fact is that what we see everywhere in the world is not only war and outbreaks of violence, we also see zones of peace and civilizing processes – even in Africa, which has become a by-word for crisis. Efforts aimed at peace have not only miscarried, there are also success stories. Human rights have experienced not only setbacks but also marked progress. And there are new approaches aimed at civilizing international relations.

'New threats' faced by the 'global risk society'

Hardly had the risk scenario of the Cold War vanished than a multiplicity of 'new threats' were identified:

- the proliferation of weapons of mass destruction in so-called 'new weapon states' which, with help from abroad – technology mercenaries from the CIS, technology hardware from the West – are in a position to develop far-reaching carrier systems;
- the threat of international terrorism, brought home to the world through attacks in a number of different places;
- internationally organized crime and the proliferation of Mafia-type subcultures ('crime import') as well as the drugs trade, organized by criminal gangs, and an increasing incidence of piracy in international shipping lanes;
- the threat posed by the 'population explosion' in the developing world, with at times frightening scenarios being painted of the inherent danger presented by this so-called 'P-bomb';
- new 'mass exoduses' in the wake of civil war and environmental disasters, population pressure and mass immiseration;
- ecological crises associated with the consequences of the greenhouse effect, increasing desertification, and the growing water scarcity to be observed in some regions of the world;
- conflicts over scarce resources such as oil, land, water, and fish stocks, and above all 'water wars' along transboundary rivers, a threat which the UN Environment Program (UNEP), is warning of emphatically;
- conflicts carried out under the cloak of cultural or religious disputes which have been overdramatized by the term 'clash of civilizations.'

The population and migration problem is now categorized as a security problem, and global environmental conflicts, with their inherent distributional conflicts over opportunities for development and competitive advantages, are seen as posing a threat that rivals earlier military conflict potentials. Think tanks specializing in security have developed concepts of an 'extended security' which, no longer restricted to military threats, also see emerging, on the world's political periphery, various types of boomerang effects that will challenge the West.

While arms spending has declined throughout the world, with armies being reduced in size and arms industries converted, in some cases this 'disarmament' has turned out to be nothing other than qualitative rearmament, centering in part on mobile 'crisis-reaction forces.' Large stocks of weapons discarded and 'scrapped' in Eastern and Western Europe have resurfaced in great quantities when wars have broken out. Wherever wars create demand for weapons, the arms trade, whether it is organized by the public or the private sector, is only too eager and quick to fill the gap. The US has initiated new, large-scale weapons programs as a means of safeguarding its military superiority and worldwide military presence. The 'new threats' are not only providing military machines and security establishments with new imagined enemies but are also generating anxiety via collective world-views – and anxiety is a poor advisor when what is called for is rational thought and action.

The attempt by former UN Secretary-General Boutros Boutros-Ghali to place the UN in a better position to prevent and deal with such conflicts, in part by developing permanent and rapidly deployable intervention forces, was scuppered by the resistance of the big powers which dominate the Security Council. Boutros-Ghali's *Agenda for Peace* disappeared, though not without some counterproductive repercussions, into the archives because it fueled a propaganda campaign in the US against the supranational ambitions of the United Nations. It was a question of power, of who was to take the role of world policeman: the UN on behalf of the international community or the US by dint of its own power or hand in hand with NATO. The ritual declarations made before the UN General Assembly, vowing to strengthen the world organization, have done nothing to prevent its strength from being further sapped. The hopes, fed by the end of the Cold War, that the United Nations might be refashioned into the architect and the pivotal point of a 'new world order' have not been fulfilled.

Development policy is sidetracked, while North–South conflict remains virulent

Nor has North–South conflict been resolved, even though the 'end of the Third World' has been proclaimed; and as the military blocs and their confrontation potential vanished, the Nonaligned Movement was disbanded, having lost its justification (Menzel 1992). The diverse collection of states commonly termed the Third World or the South has moved in such divergent directions that even the 'Group of 77' is no longer held together by common interests. At the same time the prosperity gap between Eastern and Western Europe and the CIS region has widened, giving rise to talk of a 'tiermondization' of large parts of the former Second World, that is to say, their decline to the level of Third World countries.

The global distributional conflict between islands of prosperity and regions of poverty not only confronts world politics with a moral problem, which, 30 years ago, Johan Galtung termed 'structural violence,' it is also the structural cause of a multiplicity of global problems: poverty-related environmental degradation and migration, social conflicts and political instability, fundamentalist movements fueled by social frustrations – in short, it is the reason for the present unpeaceful development of world society.

The task of conflict prevention and peacekeeping is once again moving closer to the center of thinking on development and aid policy. Since, however, conflict prevention has had a rather poor track record, the community of bilateral and multilateral donors has been forced to bolster the funds it earmarks for emergency humanitarian assistance. But the latter has also gained a bad reputation for being, in many ways, poorly organized, filling the coffers of warlords, weakening the forces devoted to self-help, and, occasionally, even for prolonging wars. The criticism voiced against doing business on the backs of the needy is leading the agencies engaged in bilateral and multilateral emergency aid to reform and rethink their long-term ideas on conflict prevention and peacekeeping with an eye to giving these concepts the place due to them as a necessary condition of development.

Once the North–South conflict had lost the secondary role it played in the East–West conflict, the non-aligned South found itself without one of its trumps, weakened in its claim to be taken seriously as a partner in conflict. At the same time the end of the geostrategic logic of the Cold War, which had infiltrated every nook and cranny of the world, left development policy without a good measure of the political impetus that previously informed it. For the West the 'tiermondization' of Eastern Europe, with its concomitant potential migration pressure, has become a challenge 'closer to home' than crises in Africa or Asia. In addition, the growing criticism of the meager successes of development aid as well as fiscal problems in the OECD countries have contributed to a situation marked by shrinking foreign aid budgets.

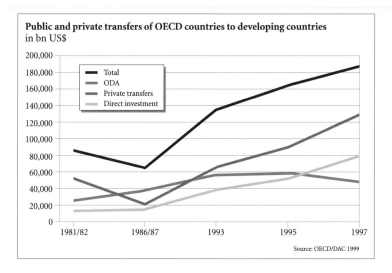

Figure 5.2

Two facts worthy of note in this connection are the sharp decline in the transfers made by the US – now only 0.9 per cent of US gross national product – and the emergence of Japan as the 'world ODA champion.' But since 1996 Japan too has been cutting its foreign aid budget (see Figure 5.3).

While it is true that the volume of private foreign direct investment has increased substantially, these investments are for the most part concentrated in ten Newly Industrialized Countries (NICs) in East and Southeast Asia and Latin America; and in 1998 these investments declined abruptly in the wake of the financial crises besetting the emerging markets. The World Bank calculated that, in 1998, ODA transfers for all developing countries – which include the Eastern European countries in transformation – amounted to only one-sixth of the volume of the funds mobilized by the International Monetary Fund (IMF) from bilateral and multilateral sources for rescue actions in Brazil, Indonesia, Russia, South Korea, and Thailand. On the other hand, the IMF has had considerable difficulties raising sufficient funding for the new fund for Highly Indebted Poor Countries (HIPCs).

It is true that the 'Asia crisis' reduced flows of private capital to Asia, cutting into the economic performance record of the 'Tiger Economies.' But while the latter have good prospects for recovery,

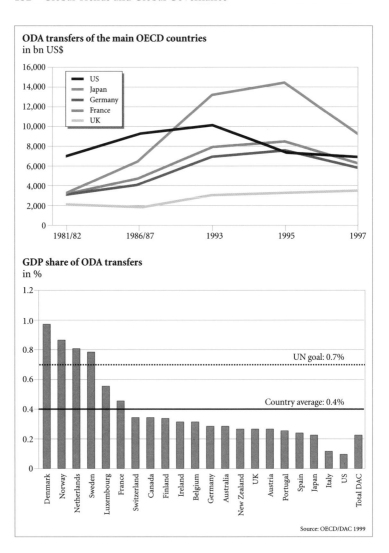

Figure 5.3

the (at present) 48 Least Developed Countries (LLDCs), most of them
located in Subsaharan Africa and already categorized as HIPCs, are
likely to prove to be the losers of globalization. Their share of world
social product, world trade, and international investment capital has
already shrunk to a residual value. At the same time their foreign

debt has become, in the words of the World Bank, an 'intolerable burden.' The LLDCs have also been marginalized in world politics, and they are often stigmatized as international welfare cases.

The North–South conflict remains a potent source of turbulence in international politics, with the South and its restless political and social landscape remaining a source of world-political turmoil. Should the North–South prosperity divide widen in the coming decades, as indicated by projections based on currently visible development trends, this prognosis would become far more likely.

The challenge of a constructive North–South policy also means seeing those unable to keep up with the pace of the world economy not as disruptive factors but as partners, whose cooperation is essential in dealing with a variety of 'new threats.' Development policy must be conceived as a global structural policy capable of drawing the necessary consequences from the fact that the 'global risk society' is a community of shared risks and shared responsibilities, one that must assume responsibility for the weakest members of the world – if not out of solidarity, then out of the recognition that the impoverishment of entire regions is likely to have repercussions for the world as a whole. The action programs adopted by the most recent world conferences prove that what is lacking is not landmark proposals but the political will to translate them into practice.

Shifting conceptions of the world: a multipolar or a unipolar world order?

The 1991 issue of *Global Trends* illustrated the shift in thinking in world politics following the end of the period of bipolarity. In reducing the world to manageable scenarios, ideologies and world-views seek to bring a measure of transparency to the 'new intransparency,' though they do remain subjective and frequently distort reality. They take on political weight not only by shaping collective attitudes, prejudices, and fears, but also by seeking to influence the action of political leadership groups.

The picture of a 'multipolar world,' often painted following the breakdown of the bipolar macro-constellation, was intended to give expression to the fact that new regional power centers were emerging alongside the existing leading powers. This multipolar view of the world centered on the growth of the world-economic significance of Japan and the European Union (EU), as well as on the growing political clout of regional powers such as China and India, countries which together account for over one-third of the world's population. Both these nations have nuclear weapons and carrier systems and are engaged in a tense arms race with neighboring countries.

This picture of a 'multipolar world' did, however, tend to mask the power-based hierarchical order of the world's states and the rise of the US as the only world power capable of global action, and the US, under the Clinton administration, resolutely pursued a policy of hegemony. The US has weakened the UN system by refusing to pay its contributions, balking on several occasions at joining international regimes, including the climate and landmine conventions and the International Court of Justice, ignoring the ban on the use of force enshrined in the UN Charter, and generally acting in accordance with the maxim: as much unilateralism as possible, as much multilateralism as necessary in the national interest.

Academic and public discussion in the US is once again dominated by a 'realist school' which, informed by the Gulf War and the Bosnian conflict, has refused to rule out the possibility of further wars, continuing to subscribe to the maxim that military might is the necessary prerequisite of its superpower status. This has made the US the cornerstone of a 'unipolar world.' Zbigniew Brzezinski (1997) referred to the US as the 'only world power,' one based on four crucial domains of global power: worldwide military presence, worldwide economic and technological leadership, and cultural hegemony.

Yet this hegemonic claim to world leadership, and the self-image of the 'only world power' deriving from it, are not uncontroversial. Paul Kennedy (1988) countered with his thesis that the US was already in the phase of 'imperial overstretching' and that a pentarchy of new power centers was emerging – the US, plus the EU, Japan, China, and Russia. Indeed, over a decade later, there are still a number of world-political realities and trends that refute the US's claim to unipolar hegemony.

In the first place, the *Pax Americana* is a shaky order in that the world policeman, the US, is neither willing nor able to police the entire world and keep world peace. Peacekeeping is inconceivable without international cooperation and the legal mandate that only the UN Security Council can bestow. In the second place, a hegemonic politics that demands obedience also invites resistance and the formation of anti-hegemonic alliances (between Russia and China, for example); it may also intensify efforts aimed at establishing a counter-power by organizing regional cooperation and integration projects. The launch of the euro in the EU was not only a monetary but also a political project. Claims to cultural hegemony may also mobilize the kind of defense reactions that Samuel P. Huntington (1996) has dramatized as a 'clash of civilizations.'

Third, while the US is the only country today with the military potential of a global world power, it is no longer has economic and political hegemony. The world has become so transnationally inter-dependent that even a military superpower cannot, in the long run, be in a position to maintain a 'unipolar world order.' A 'judgment of Solomon' was offered by Huntington (1999, p. 36). He characterized the international system as a 'uni-multipolar system' with one superpower and several big powers. He noted at the same time that the 'lonely superpower' was increasingly forced to seek international cooperation.

In the emerging era of geo-economics and the geo-economy – that is, the era of a growing economization of international relations – it is no longer, as in the era of geopolitics, military power alone that determines the ranking of nations in global competition, but tech-nological potential and systemic competitiveness too. This geo-economy constitutes the framework in which the world-economic triad and the 'trilateral view of the world' have emerged. The architecture of the triad gave birth to the G7, which has developed from a loose consultation forum into a 'world economic summit' and an instrument of world crisis management. This 'club of the rich and powerful' also has the say in the international financial organizations (the IMF and World Bank) that, by means of their lending conditionalities, heavily influence the economic and social policies of debtor countries, advancing as they do the neoliberal project of a world market economy. The enlargement of the G7 to form a G8 by the inclusion of Russia was a political gesture to involve Russia as a major military power in international crisis management – a move, it must be noted, that came much too late in the Kosovo conflict.

The 'trilateral view of the world' rests on the assumption that the 'OECD world' of the western industrialized states, which are held together by a high level of economic interdependence and political coordination, is not only the world's center of economic gravity but also its political navel. One of its strengths lies in the fact that it transformed itself from a theater of war to a zone of peace which, while marked by conflicts over power and trade issues, has been able to resolve its conflicts peacefully. Seen in terms of civilizing inter-national relations, this world has reached a high degree of maturity.

Here we see the realization of one of the central assumptions of peace theory: that interdependence serves peace.

Today's world order consists of a mixture of different models, which is depicted in Figure 5.4 in the form of ideal types. It contains an underlying hegemonic element, but the UN Security Council, instrumentalized though it may be by hegemonic interests, amounts to the building block, functionally restricted as it may be, of a world state. This world order also seeks to reduce the anarchy of the world of states by involving them in a regime of horizontal self-coordination achieved through international organizations and regimes.

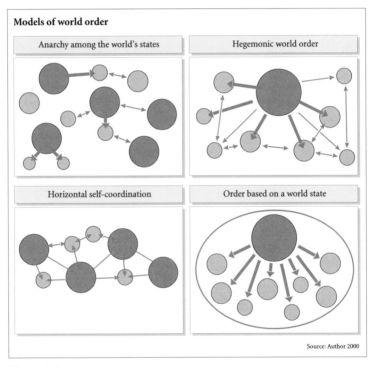

Models of world order

Anarchy among the world's states

Hegemonic world order

Horizontal self-coordination

Order based on a world state

Source: Author 2000

Figure 5.4

The European Union: a major economic power and a regional political power

The 'OECD world,' which now includes two NICs – Mexico and South Korea – has not only experienced the creation of a large new economic space, the European Union, which is now set to expand eastward, it has also seen the emergence of a new cultural, legal, and social space with an effective supranational jurisdiction. The EU is already a major economic power with a common international economic policy of its own. When the euro was introduced as its currency, the EU also became a world monetary power. But in terms of world politics its scope of action is limited, because the EU's project of a Common Foreign and Security Policy (CFSP) is making only gradual progress.

The EU's development policy, the part of its CFSP directed toward the South, also suffers from competition between special national interests. The future of the Lomé Convention, which, with its combination of development aid and trade preferences, constitutes the core of the EU's development policy, is uncertain, because the trade preferences extended to the Lomé partners conflict in some ways with the World Trade Organization's (WTO) principles of free trade. All in all the European Development Fund may not have been as successful as it might have been. EU-Europe does, however, have a special historical responsibility to its former colonies and must therefore look for new approaches to cooperation. This also goes for the EU's Mediterranean policy, which focuses on a conflict-laden space which constitutes the arena of the encounter between Orient and Occident and is at the same time a flash-point and a point of intersection for South–North migration.

Thanks to the fact that the CFSP has not proved wholly workable, the EU itself has been forced to fall back on the political leadership of the US and the military potential of NATO in coming to terms with the conflict in the Balkans. The Organization for Security and Cooperation in Europe (OSCE), saddled with inflated expectations following the dismantling of the Iron Curtain, has, in view of the security framework in Europe, been unable to play more than a marginal, albeit quite useful, role in dealing with European conflicts. But the Balkans saw the failure of the concept of an 'OSCE Europe' that sought to find European solutions for conflicts in the OSCE region.

In his geostrategic thinking, Henry Kissinger (1994) saw a role for the EU as a political world power only if it succeeded in deepening its integration and finding its way to an effective common foreign and security policy (CFSP). This qualitative leap in integration would, however, presuppose the integration of the Western European Union (WEU) into the EU, alongside the search for a common defense policy and the development of capacities for military action. The limited capacity to act which has beset both EU and OSCE in their interventions in the Balkan crises stepped up the pressure to develop the CFSP, to build a European security profile, and to integrate the CIS region and the countries of south-eastern Europe in a European security structure. In May 1999, the WEU, under the pressure of the war in the Balkans, decided to get on with the job, anchored in the Treaty of Amsterdam, of integrating the EU and WEU, using this functional symbiosis as a means of developing a European capacity to act in security matters while at the same time of boosting the EU's weight in NATO.

Alternative peace concepts that see, and wish to strengthen, Europe as a civilian power sustained a setback in the Balkans that will not quickly be forgotten. The peace movement was confronted with the dilemma of either responding to genocide and mass expulsion with ineffectual moral outrage or reluctantly accepting the use of force and violence. In the twenty-first century the EU will not only have to come to terms with its expansion to the east, it will also have to redefine its role in transatlantic relations and in world politics. The EU's concern is to make its multilateral foreign policy credo heard in international relations and vis-à-vis the unilateralism favored by the US.

The world of regions and cultures

The new configuration of world-economic and world-political weights, the 'multipolar world,' has been accompanied by a process of regionalization that has been intensified by the pressure exerted by globalization. All regions are experiencing the formation of zones of cooperation or integration. These are based on geographic proximity and shared cultural features, though they also serve the end of joint self-assertion in the face of an increasingly globalized world, one understood in many quarters as a threat to political autonomy, cultural identity, and economic competitiveness. Now that the East–West conflict is over, many international relations analysts have noted the formation of a 'regionalized world,' which offers greater scope for action to regional actors. Such regionaliza-tion tendencies have come about not only in economic and cultural affairs but also in the area of security (Lake and Morgan 1997).

The scenario of a 'clash of civilizations' conjured up by Samuel P. Huntington – which found great resonance throughout the world – noted first and foremost that the world consists not only of economic spaces or geopolitical zones but also of cultural spaces.

Huntington's core thesis is that in the twenty-first century world politics will no longer be marked by economic or power interests; instead, the battlefield of the future will be drawn up along the lines of cultural fronts within and between states. He anticipates the emergence of such cultural conflicts at many points of contact between cultures, above all along the seams between Orient and Occident. In his construction of a new threat to the West posed by the 'rest of the world' – a surrogate for the vanished image of the Communist as enemy, and one delineating a new bipolarity – Huntington proved himself blind to several causes of the retreat of politics behind the veil of culture and religion as well as of the growing strength of fundamentalist movements.

In the first place, cultures or religions do not wage war against one another; rather, they are used as political weapons in internal power struggles and as an instrument of mass mobilization. Such 'wars of religion' tend to take place above all in multi-ethnic societies torn apart by social or political crises – as we saw, for instance, in 1998/99 in Indonesia. In the second place, the sources from which the fundamentalist 'revolt against modernity' are fed include mainly development crises and social frustrations, neither of which can be effectively engaged with arms drawn. The 'holy war' needs an enemy, and needs to clothe that enemy in religious trappings, though the source of the phenomenon is clearly of a political and social nature.

In the third place, the recourse to religion in fundamentalist circles, the so-called religious revival, is a reaction to globalization processes, which are interpreted as a 'westernization' entailing the loss of cultural identity. In fact, it is a response to uncertainties in a situation of sociocultural upheaval. This counter-tendency to globalization also finds expression in a 'new regionalism' and localism, in a search for micro-spaces and a sense of community. This process and the dialectic driving it have been termed, perhaps unhappily, as 'glocalization.'

In the fourth place, many conflicts that appear in the guise of cultural clashes should be interpreted as decolonization conflicts or as defense reactions against the West's political, economic, and cultural hegemony. The 'Asianism' to be found in Confucian cultures or the emphasis sometimes placed on 'Asian values' has little to do with the value codex of Confucius. They are more an expression of a new self-confidence born in the shelter of economic successes and the wish to see a 'Pacific century' supersede the 'American century'.

Huntington provoked much criticism, which has been compiled in a 'counter-project' and which led Dieter Senghaas (1998: 135ff.) to dismiss the scenario of an international clash of civilizations as an 'idée fixe.'

Figure 5.5

Huntington's world of civilizations is largely in accord with the world map of civilizations published in 1990 by *The Economist* (see Figure 5.5). It pushes the Occident closely together (Western Europe and North America with its 'appendage' Latin America), dividing Europe along historical-cultural lines that split the Balkans and run along a line defined by a NATO expanded to the east. It lumps together the 'Islamic world,' which extends from Morocco to Indonesia, to form an 'Islamistan,' and it fuses all of East Asia to form a virtual 'Confuciania.'

What is noteworthy here is not just that the cartographers have conjured Subsaharan African off the face of the map, apparently seeing in it neither any autonomous cultures nor any world-political relevance. Their picture of the world enlarges Euro-America in keeping with such world-political relevance criteria and diminishes the size of 'Hinduland,' which will soon catch up with China as the world's most populous country. What, however, is even more noteworthy is the fact that the world map suggests a drifting apart of cultural regions. Globalization, in contrast, draws them together – a process that has been expressed in the image of 'One World.'

The concurrence of globalization and regionalization is one of the structure-building trends of world society and world politics alike. Globalization will see the emergence of a new hierarchy of the world's regions, it will further strengthen the 'OECD world,' and will decouple the world's poor regions from the dynamics of the world economy. It will at the same time open up new opportunities for core countries in Latin America and East and Southeast Asia. While the Asia crisis may have delayed the dawn of the 'Pacific century,' thereby prolonging the 'American century's' lease on life, the rise of the China (a nuclear power) as a major economic power means both a shift of weight in East Asia and a modification of the 'trilateral view of the world.' Despite the profound structural and economic crisis it faced in the 1990s, and notwithstanding many an over-hasty adieu, Japan will remain a major economic and technological power, while China is rising to the status of a major political and military power. The major steps it is taking toward boosting its military capabilities have already led to new security-related containment strategies under the leadership of the US.

New structural elements of world politics in the 'age of globalism'

The new century, despite world-political turbulence, promises to be an age of globalism, one marked by the following development tendencies and structural elements.

A new quality of globalization

The significance and scope of globalization remain controversial. Globalization has long since become one of the most used and misused slogans in circulation. There is, however, no controversy over whether or not there are more transboundary interactions interlocking all countries and societies in a complex system of mutual interdependence, though one marked by different degrees of vulnerability.

Interdependence in the 'global risk society' means that both states and societies are less and less able to distance themselves from international development trends. Civil wars in the Balkans lead to flows of refugees to Western Europe, contribute to domestic conflicts there, and set an intervention mechanism in train. The collapse of a hedge fund gives rise to turbulence in the global financial markets.

Greenhouse gases deplete the ozone layer and endanger the world climate, whether they are emitted in China or in Western Europe.

The new quality of globalization consists in the fact that it not only intensifies the interdependencies and mutual vulnerabilities between countries, but that it also narrows the scope for maneuver open to governments in many policy fields. Three circumstances are chiefly responsible for this. First, the growing mobility of firms and capital leads to a structural imbalance between government and economy, which in turn stimulates competition between industrial locations and narrows the scope of political action in fiscal, social, and environmental policy. Second, many of the problems experienced by nation-states have external causes and very often exceed the ability of national governments to find solutions to them. Third, globalization could contribute to a situation in which domestic stability and the legitimation of democratic institutions come under considerable pressure. This is why Ralf Dahrendorf has warned of an impending 'authoritarian century.' The transboundary quality of many problems is forcing governments to seek international co-operation in their own enlightened self-interest.

Shift in the substance of sovereignty

For states and societies alike one of the consequences of globalization is a blurring of boundaries and processes of 'denationalization,' and these entail shifts in the substance of sovereignty. The latter is eroded by expanding and increasingly dense spheres of interdependence and transnational interaction. While, in the world of international law, sovereignty will continue to be the constitutive principle of the nation-state, in the real world of international relations the concept of sovereignty is, ultimately, an anachronism. Nation-states no longer have the unrestricted freedom of action attributed to them in Hobbes's *Leviathan.* The crucial question today is how nation-states can still be ruled in increasingly less clearly delimited spaces and how, under these circumstances, they are to retain their capacity to formulate policy and solve problems.

Nation-states will have to come to terms with a 'divided sovereignty' which leaves them their domestic monopoly of power while depriving them of that measure of their external sovereignty that is needed collectively to process problems resulting from interdependence. This is true especially in the sphere of security policy, the core element of any assertion of national power and interests. True, the UN still has no monopoly on the use of force, but the Security

Council does have the exclusive right to authorize and legitimize its use, a right that was certainly shaken *de facto* by NATO's intervention in Kosovo, but one which nevertheless is not generally a matter of dispute. A 'culture of intervention' has for some time now been everyday practice in development and human rights. There is thus a certain tension between the prohibition on interference in a state's internal affairs as codified in Article 2(7) of the UN Charter and the mandate of the international community, set out in Article 2(3), to protect and foster human rights.

Shift in the role of the nation-state

The nation-state is and will remain the main actor in international politics. It alone is able to establish international legal norms, and it has the final say in all disputes and points of contention, unless – as in the case of the EU – a group of states have resolved to submit to a set of supranational decision mechanisms. But nation-states no longer have the free hand they had at the Vienna Congress; they are

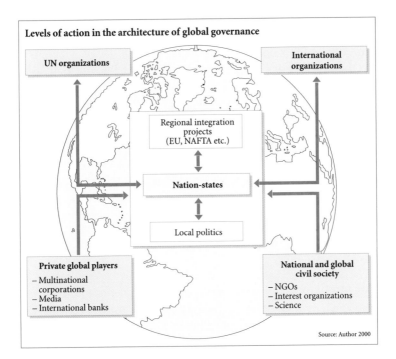

Levels of action in the architecture of global governance

UN organizations

International organizations

Regional integration projects (EU, NAFTA etc.)

Nation-states

Local politics

Private global players
– Multinational corporations
– Media
– International banks

National and global civil society
– NGOs
– Interest organizations
– Science

Source: Author 2000

Figure 5.6

no longer able control policy fields that have been caught up in the current of globalization processes. The nation-state is no longer the all-powerful Leviathan responsible for all things, nor is it damned to powerlessness or at the end of its *raison d'être*, as some book titles suggest. But its role in world politics is shifting (Messner 1998).

Nation-states will remain responsible for authoritative decisions, for implementing the decisions taken at the international level, and for coordinating various groups of actors at the national and international levels (see Figure 5.6). Their integration into a system of 'divided sovereignties' thus does not diminish their capacities to formulate policy; in fact, it is a prerequisite for securing governance and policy-making capacities under the conditions of globalization.

The traditional billiard ball model of international politics, still pervasive in the way nation-states view the world, has long since given way to a web-based model of a multiplicity of interlinkages beyond traditional international diplomacy. International relations in transnational spaces are far more comprehensive and multilayered than the acts of nation-states. While the nation-state remains the main pillar of global governance, it is in need of further pillars and network-like elements that will tie it into the world of economy and society if it is not to lose its ability to act.

One cardinal question is how – in view of the fact that some important decisions are being removed from the sphere of competence of the nation-state and are now to be entrusted to international bureaucrats – we are to approach and solve the problems of democracy and democratic legitimation. The solution can be neither the participation of non-governmental organizations (NGOs) in consultation mechanisms, nor a 'democratization' of international organizations, since the latter can do no more than provide for a broad representation of states. Proposals aimed at expanding assemblies of representatives of states to include 'popular representations' pose organizational and efficiency problems. The democratization of multilateralism is thus a central problem of global governance.

The multilateralism constraint

The challenges posed by global problems are forcing countries to intensify their international cooperation, a fact that not even a hegemon in a 'unipolar world' can afford to ignore. While in view of its extensive power a hegemonic state may prefer unilateralism, it cannot get along without some measure of international cooperation and burden-sharing. Subject to the pressure of the problems posed by the 'global risk society,' the final decades of the twentieth century may be termed the 'age of international organizations and regimes.' As Figure 5.1 illustrates, this period saw a proliferation of the number of international organizations that took the stage as new actors in international politics, organizing modes of international cooperation and horizontal self-regulation in their capacity as inter-governmental organizations (IGOs).

The most important new approach to a regulation of trans-boundary problems, and one leading to a new focus in the theory of international relations, has been the international regime. Here countries come to an agreement on common interests and goals, sets of durable and binding rules which are the result of the pressure of problems that one state alone is no longer able to master. Some such regimes are of a regional nature – for instance the Rhine or the Baltic Sea regimes – others, like the World Trade Organization – are of global scope. Even the major powers are willing to accept such regimes because they see no other way of solving problems that have serious repercussions for them. The turbulences in the international financial markets following the 'Asia crisis' have moved western politicians and finance experts, bankers, and even big speculators of the caliber of George Soros to think about the need for an interna-tional regulatory regime for the financial sector. It was the pressure engendered by problems, not theories, that brought about this reori-entation in thinking.

'NGOization of world politics'?

Global governance is often translated as more multilateralism, that is, it is seen as a strengthening and intensification of international cooperation in international organizations. The journal *Global Governance* reflects this understanding of the matter in its subtitle *A Review of Multilateralism and International Organizations*. But the concept of global governance, which was worked out by the Commission on Global Governance and is best understood to mean 'world regulative policy,' goes one substantial step further. Proceeding from the experience that in many policy fields the state is forced to seek cooperation with social groups, the Commission sees the qualitatively new element underlying global governance in the collaboration between governmental and non-governmental actors at all levels of action. It emphasized above all the growing sig-nificance of multinational corporations, of media corporations, for instance, that, using the means provided by global telecommunications, penetrate the ether above international boundaries, as well as of NGOs with their increasingly transnational networks.

The collaborative and policy-shaping role of these NGOs at the world conferences of the 1990s, the active role played by human rights organizations in international human rights policy, the initiative role of worldwide NGO campaigns in bringing about the international convention against landmines, and the influence of environmental groups on national and international environmental policy have posed the question whether we are faced with a *fait accompli* – the 'NGOization of world politics' – which has seen NGOs gradually penetrate the circle of international law. UN Secretary-General Kofi Annan (1998) has spoken of a 'quiet revolution' behind the scenes of the world of states. Jessica Mathews (1996), president of the influential Carnegie Endowment for International Peace, sees a 'power shift' in the relation between state and civil society.

On the one hand, for hard-boiled statists in foreign ministries and for 'realists' in international relations, the 'rag-tag assemblages' that are NGOs still constitute a bothersome, vociferous, though ultimately impotent, troublemaker potential in the exclusive sphere of action and competence populated by states and their diplomats. What we find, on the other hand, is a whole new genre of literature that casts NGOs in the elevated role of the leaven of world society and fountain of youth of world politics. For Habermas (1999b) it will not be states but civic movements that bring about the democratic reshaping of the world. The assessment of their role in international relations varies between an uncritical romanticization that may sometimes even encourage a certain self-overestimation on the part of NGOs and a more or less scornful disregard. Both extremes do injustice to NGOs.

It is important to distinguish the policy fields in which NGOs are for the most part active. In the policy fields of human rights, the environment, and development they have succeeded in using their transnational networks to put states under pressure to prove their legitimacy and to act. The most recent world conferences showed that far from being relegated to the back seat of international negotiations, as they used to be, NGOs are now in some cases incorporated into government delegations. This is an instance of global governance in practice. On the other hand, NGOs play a more or less marginal role in foreign and security policy; though here too – for instance, in the fields of conflict prevention, mediation, and humanitarian aid – states are often happy to avail themselves of the services provided by NGOs. It is not through an 'NGOization of world politics,' but by means of a juridification and civilization of international relations, a task that only states can accomplish, that a truly 'new world order' may come about. But NGOs are an active force working in the direction of change by opposing their vision of a 'globalization from the bottom up' to any top-down versions of globalization. Their *engagement* for global public goods is an important element in the development of a world ethics, the normative foundation of global governance.

The global governance project: perspectives

We can distinguish several different approaches in the discussion over whether and how it is possible actively to shape the course of globalization. A small number of 'globalists' cling to their vision of a world state. A 'world King Kong' of this kind is, however, an option that is neither realistic nor desirable in that a bureaucratic moloch of this sort could hardly be expected to acquire the democratic legitimation it would need to play its role as the *deus ex machina* needed to solve world problems. A world social council, or an IMF upgraded to the function of a world central bank, would suffer from the structural weaknesses and lack of efficiency that plague centralism and bureacratism. Worldwide, decentralization is high on the agenda of political reform. The democratic imperative is bottom up instead of top down! Kant's vision of a federation of free republics still has landmark character.

An expanding group of authors, whose concerns have found expression in different concepts, regard a cooperative global governance architecture as essential to halt the growing impotence of politics in the face of the dynamics inherent to globalization processes. They are thinking here above all of the phenomenon known as 'casino capitalism.' The Group of Lisbon (1997), for instance, argues in favor of a global social, cultural, earth, and democracy pact as a means of organizing the emerging world society in accordance with viable social, ecological, and democratic principles. Such projects, with their different names and emphases, are based on similar presuppositions and outlines:

1. A global governance architecture would be polycentric, because the world of states, the world of regions and cultures, is polycentric and any attempt to ignore this would be doomed to

failure. The key question is how to overcome the blockade of cooperative action constituted by the power differential in the international system.

2. Global governance rests on different forms and levels of international coordination, cooperation, and collective decision-making. International organizations exercise such functions, contributing to the emergence of global modes of perception. Regimes translate the will to cooperate into sets of binding rules. Gradually, the patchwork of sectoral approaches may give rise to a quilt of cooperative structures.

3. Global governance is not restricted to more multilateralism at the global level. Many problems call for political responses at different levels of action, from the local to the global. There are climate protection measures that must be coordinated at the international level, implemented at the national level, and enforced at the local level. Agenda 21, adopted by the 1992 Rio Conference on Environment and Development, contains a 'local Agenda 21' that, throughout the world, has set in motion local initiatives aimed at more sustainability in different areas of life.

4. Global governance casts the traditional view of sovereignty in the light of an anachronistic relict of a world of states that has long since ceased to exist. The constraint to cooperate calls for partner states formally to relinquish some of their sovereign rights, an effect that has already been brought about by the course of globalization. To be able to engage in global cooperation, the major powers will have to accept a world of 'divided sovereignties,' which, as the EU demonstrates, can in the end mean enhanced capacities for action and problem-solving and more chances to actively shape world politics.

5. Global governance calls for the reorganization of government machinery and institutional innovation, because all policy fields – including domestic policy, that is, internal security, immigration, and asylum – are tied into global contexts. The task facing us is to focus isolated fields of ministerial competence to form effective policy networks, but also to give individual policy fields a new orientation. For instance, development policy should a) be coordinated more at the international level; and b) be further developed from a series of isolated projects into a global structural policy that subjects all policy fields to the imperatives of sustainability and cooperation. While this would entail sub-

stantial effort aimed at coordination, it would also mean gains in policy coherence.

6. Global governance is nevertheless not a project involving governments or international organizations only. The latter are in many cases reliant on the know-how of and cooperation with private actors; that is, on public–private partnership. This stems from the need to involve societal actors in solving global problems. Politics here would be organized more and more in horizontally and vertically networked structures (Messner 1997). In individual policy fields (environment, human rights, and development) NGOs would have consultative, corrective, and active roles in functions associated with the formulation of policy.

7. Global governance can and must build on something like the foundations laid by Kant in the three first definitive articles to his 'Perpetual Peace.' First, peace secure in the long run can come about only in and between states constituted under the rule of law. Second, while world politics does not need a governing world state, it does need the regulative force of binding international law. Third, an emerging world society must build on a 'cosmopolitan constitution' with 'cosmopolitan rights.'

Perspectives and options: superpower governance versus global governance?

The main objections to the project of global governance are twofold: either global governance serves hegemonic interests, and thereby insinuates them into international organizations and regimes; or it is blind to the power factor and is thus, in view of the real powers behind world politics, at best a Utopia for a world in the future. 'Realists' in politics and science see little likelihood that the project will be realized. They tend to see globalization as entailing situations marked by sharper competition, deregulation, and trade conflicts in the geo-economy.

As we enter the twenty-first century, global governance is still a fragile project. The Clinton administration's departure from a 'self-assured multilateralism' and its step in the direction of a hegemonic unilateralist policy that, potentially, will not stop short of dismantling of the UN system, the supporting pillar of the global governance architecture; uncertainties as to the future role of the one-time big power Russia and the rise of China as a new big power, with both of them, as permanent members of the UN Security

Council, claiming world leadership roles for themselves – all these are portentous and far-reaching development trends that characterize world politics at the threshold of the new century.

Where is world politics headed after the war in Kosovo?

NATO's decision to use military force against the rump of Yugoslavia without authorization from the UN Security Council is a turning point in international politics. NATO's intervention was motivated by the need to put an end to a humanitarian catastrophe. An additional factor was the concrete interest of the Europeans in preventing both a mass exodus of Kosovo-Albanians to the European Union and the destabilization of the Balkans. With a view to achieving these goals, the 19 NATO states ignored international law and a core element of the UN Charter – Article 2(4), the international ban on the use of force – and violated one of the principles set out in the preamble to the NATO Treaty, setting out NATO's obligation to respect the 'purposes and principles of the United Nations.'

Despite its manifest violation of international law, NATO's intervention might have been justified by reference to precisely these purposes and principles. Indeed, it might have been justified by reference to a higher right not covered by international law – the right to end a state of international emergency – in particular once it had become clear that the efforts of the Western Contact Group to find a negotiated settlement had failed. One could cite other sources of international law as a legal basis for the intervention, though without dispelling all objections: the 1948 Convention on the Prevention and Punishment of Genocide, the outlawing of 'crimes against humanity' in the principles of the war crimes tribunals and the International Criminal Court (ICC), and Resolution 688 of the UN Security Council on the protection of the Kurds in northern Iraq.

NATO's action, highly controversial as it was, was risky. For instance, it failed to achieve its declared aims on the ground, viz. to use air strikes on Serb targets as a means of stopping the expulsion of Kosovo-Albanians. The international implications were no less weighty: Russia, one of the world's major powers, was humiliated for the second time following the eastward expansion of NATO, which had revived old Russian fears of encirclement, thereby strengthening the hand of Russia's opposition and nationalist forces. The 'Partnership for Peace' was severely damaged, and Russia's decision to resume the war in Chechnya was encouraged by NATO's unauthorized bombing of Serbia. In spite of its reliance on IMF loans, Russia's domestic and foreign policy has become less predictable.

NATO's self-authorization not only undermined the UN Security Council's monopoly on mandating the use of force, it also ignored the claims of Russia and China to play an active and cooperative role in formulating world politics in terms of the joint security established in the course of the OSCE process. The world has since been faced with the threat of a new East–West conflict, one grounded not in ideology but in power politics.

Even prior to the Kosovo crisis the US had pushed for the abandonment of the principle of Security Council authorization for humanitarian interventions as well as for a worldwide expansion of NATO's field of operations. The New Strategic Concept, presented on the 50th anniversary of NATO in the spring of 1999, provided for the transformation of NATO from a purely defensive alliance into a more comprehensive security organization whose core tasks include not only the defense of the alliance but also a so-called 'out of area' crisis management. NATO's intention to go through with the Kosovo intervention, if need be without UN authorization and outside the alliance's territory, makes this action a precedent that undermines the UN Security Council's monopoly on the authorization of the use of force.

However there are factors working against any return to worldwide 'gunboat diplomacy': the risks of such interventions, made plain for example in Somalia and Kosovo; reservations on the part of NATO members about any expansion of NATO's field of operation beyond the Euro-Atlantic areas; and, above all, public opinion. The public is less 'war-happy' than inclined to keep out of conflicts 'across the world.' As the presidential campaign in the US demonstrates, the readiness shown in the 1990s to intervene militarily for purely humanitarian reasons has strongly diminished, and the Republicans in particular are more reluctant than ever to be drawn into wars by the so-called CNN factor (Rice 2000).

The dilemma – also as seen from the perspective of global governance – is that the project of civilizing international relations includes containing violence and severe human rights violations. In other words, the question in Kosovo was whether, at the heart of Europe, victory would belong to 'bestiality or humanity,' as Habermas (1999a) put it in assessing this 'war on the boundary between law and morality.' Seen in terms of a conflict between norms, the basic right of a people to exist ranks higher than international law, a law of states. At present the veto of a single member of the UN Security Council is sufficient to prevent the authorization of a humanitarian intervention. But the response to this cannot be a situation in which an intervention-minded group of countries simply creates its own ad hoc right to intervene, misusing 'humanitarian interventionism' as a means of circumventing the UN Charter.

One way out of this dilemma might to strengthen regional organizations such as OSCE, OAS, or OAU in conflict management. However, in this case Chapter VII of the UN Charter would have to be amended to include an appropriate empowerment clause. The essential thing would be to create – whether at the global or at the regional level – an intervention regime that would close the regulative gap under international law between international protection of human rights and the ban on intervention, while at the same time closing the door on arbitrary intervention. Under the conditions of interdependence and seen in terms of the normative criteria of universal human rights, Article 2(7) of the UN Charter, the universal ban on intervention is an anachronistic relict from the 'world of yesteryear.' It needs to be amended, just as the UN Security Council does. For here, following the Second World War, the victorious powers cemented their right of veto. Reform of the UN system remains an urgent task of international politics, one that can once again ensure that the founding principles of the United Nations are respected and the institution is in a position to play its central role in the architecture of global governance.

In the 'age of globalism' the international community cannot stand idly by when a return to barbarism is threatened anywhere in the world. The United Nations has always been successful here, and will, after the negative experiences made in the last decade, continue to be so, as long as no vital interests of leading world powers or regional powers are involved – as, for instance, in the case of Subsaharan Africa. The manner in which, at present, the UN's authority to keep the peace is being undermined could encourage the re-emergence of anarchic tendencies in international relations. If the concept of world domestic policy is to be meaningful, a 'political culture of legitimate intervention' must be developed. Habermas (1999a) has called for a cosmopolitan right that would ensure that the use of force in favor of persecuted individuals and peoples does not remain a moral question only but becomes a duty under the law. Such demands could and should lead to a more comprehensive 'culture of peace' (Galtung 1996).

Weapons can at best prevent the worst; they cannot create a durable peace. Peace enforcement is followed by the more difficult task of peace-building. The Stability Pact for Southeast Europe points in the right direction. In terms of an 'ex post facto prevention' (Rohloff 2000), the European Union is trying its hand at crisis prevention by exporting stability. Reconstruction aid, inter-regional economic promotion, and consolidation of the forces of civil society on the ground are to be used to lead southeastern Europe, in the medium and long term, into the state of democracy and peace characteristic of the OECD world. But it is not only for European conflicts that it will be essential to make more intensive use of the opportunities offered by the instruments of peaceful conflict-processing. The proposals contained in the *Agenda for Peace* must be liberated from the UN archives.

Global governance: a future perspective

At the threshold of the new century the founding purpose of the United Nations and the world system of collective security are in for a severe test. There has long been more talk of a 'new world disorder' than of a new world order in which not power but international law and a culture of cooperation determine the actions of states. Superpower governance seems to have won the day over global governance. It is still not possible to say 'where the world is headed.'

Nevertheless there are developments that indicate that global governance is more than an illusion: the establishment of a number of regimes that are deepening international cooperation in various policy fields; the creation of an International Criminal Court authorized to persecute crimes against humanity throughout the world; the emergence of an international civil society ('cosmopolitan society') unwilling to leave politics to states; and the attempt of world conferences to reach cooperative solutions to the world's most urgent problems. Many positive steps, such as improvement of the protection of human rights or the development of a maritime regime aimed at the sustainable exploitation of maritime resources, have not been sufficiently appreciated.

There will be social and ecological improvements to the WTO's trade regime and an international financial regime designed to rein in 'casino capitalism,' because the pressure deriving from concrete problems is leading to a regulation of the unruly dynamics inherent in globalization. But even such positive moves are no more than hesitant steps on the path to global governance. Political realism forbids speculation on whether the project could be advanced without – or indeed even against the will of – the world-political hegemon. It is more realistic to expect that problems will force the US too to return to multilateralism, since it will be unable to solve the problem of governability on its own or together with NATO or the G7 – and because it has become the central problem facing the international community of states (Dror 1994). Even the 'realist' Huntington (1999) has been unable to recognize any alternative to multilateralism for the 'lonely superpower,' the US.

Global governance is not a romantic project for One World, sound and intact, but a realistic response to the challenges posed by globalization and 'global risks.' This is why the unrealistic thinkers are not those who are intent on more international cooperation and an end to uncooperative hegemonic politics, but those defending the status quo, resting as it does on a transient constellation of power. Global governance is an evolutionary project, one that is advancing step by step. In spite of numerous setbacks, the preconditions for a new world order are better at the threshold of the new century than they were when the League of Nations and the United Nations were founded. The 'age of globalism' has already begun.

References

Albert, Mathias et al. (eds) (2000) *Civilizing World Politics. Society and Community beyond the State*, Oxford.

Annan, Kofi (1998) 'The Quiet Revolution,' *Global Governance*, Vol. 4(2), pp. 123–38.

Brzezinski, Zbigniew (1997) *The Grand Chessboard. American Primacy and its Geostrategic Imperatives*, New York.

Commission on Global Governance (1995) *Our Global Neighbourhood*, Oxford.

Czempiel, Ernst-Otto (1992, 2nd edition) *Weltpolitik im Umbruch*, Munich.

Dror, Yehezkel (1994) *The Capacity to Govern. A Report to the Club of Rome*, Barcelona.

Galtung, Johan (1996) *Peace by Peaceful Means*, London.

Group of Lisbon (1997) *Limits of Competition*, Cambridge, Mass.

Habermas, Jürgen (1999a) 'Bestialität und Humanität,' *Die Zeit*, No. 18 (April, 29).

Habermas, Jürgen (1999b) *Die postnationale Konstellation*, Frankfurt/M.

Hewson, Martin and Sinclair, Timothy J. (eds) (1999) *Approaches to Global Governance Theory*, New York.

Huntington, Samuel P. (1996) *The Clash of Civilizations and the Remaking of World Order*, New York.

Huntington, Samuel P. (1999) 'The Lonely Superpower,' *Foreign Affairs*, Vol. 78(2), pp. 35–49.

Kaplan, Robert (1996) *The Ends of the Earth. From Togo to Turkmenistan, from Iran to Cambodia. A Journey to the Frontiers of Anarchy*, New York.

Kennedy, Paul (1988) *The Rise and Fall of the Great Powers*, New York.

Kissinger, Henry (1994) *Die sechs Säulen der Weltordnung*, Berlin.

Lake, David A. and Patrick M. Morgan (eds.) (1997) *Regional Orders: Building Security in a New World*, University Park.

Link, Werner (1998) *Die Neuordnung der Weltpolitik. Grundprobleme globaler Politik an der Schwelle zum 21. Jahrhundert*, Munich.

Mathews, Jessica T. (1996) 'Power Shift,' *Foreign Affairs*, Vol. 76(1), pp. 50–66.

Menzel, Ulrich (1992) *Das Ende der Dritten Welt und das Scheitern der großen Theorie*, Frankfurt/M.

Menzel, Ulrich (1998) *Globalisierung versus Fragmentierung*, Frankfurt/M.

Messner, Dirk (1997) *The Network Society*, London.

Messner, Dirk (ed.) (1998) *Die Zukunft des Staates und der Politik*, Bonn.

Moynihan, Daniel Patrick (1993) *Pandaemonium: Ethnicity in International Politics*, Oxford.

OECD/DAC (Organization for Economic Cooperation and Development/ Development Assistance Committee) (1999) *Development Cooperation Report 1998*, Paris, pp. 46–7.

Rice, Condoleezza (2000) 'Promoting the National Interest,' *Foreign Affairs*, Vol. 79(1), pp. 45–62.

Rohloff, Christoph (2000) 'Nachholende Prävention: Der Stabilitätspakt für Südosteuropa,' *Friedensgutachten 2000*, Münster/Hamburg, pp. 139–48.

Rosenau, James N. and Durfee, Mary (2000, 2nd edition) *Thinking Theory Thoroughly: Coherent Approaches to an Incoherent World*, Boulder, CO.

Rufin, Jean-Christophe (1996) *Die neuen Barbaren. Der Nord-Süd-Konflikt nach dem Ende des Kalten Krieges*, Munich.

Senghaas, Dieter (1994) *Wohin driftet die Welt?* Frankfurt/M.

Senghaas, Dieter (1998) *Zivilisierung wider Willen*, Frankfurt/M.

UIA (Union of International Associations) (ed.) (1996) *Yearbook of International Organizations. Guide to Global Civil Society Networks*, Munich, p.1684.

UIA (Union of International Associations) (ed.) (1997) *Yearbook of International Organizations. Guide to Global Civil Society Networks*, Munich, p.1763.

Weiss, Thomas G. (ed.) (1997) *NGOs, the UN and Global Governance*, Boulder, CO.

6
Global Governance, Development, and Peace

Franz Nuscheler

The new world-political era which began in 1989/90 heralded the 'age of globalism.' Since then we have experienced a rapidly proliferating number of publications, countless conferences throughout the world, blueprints for the future prepared by academic think tanks and international organizations, as well as numerous ceremonial addresses dealing with the far-reaching structural changes that are affecting all spheres of life and have been reduced to the overused, not to say hackneyed, common denominator of 'globalization.' Several contributions in the present volume point, from different perspectives, to the concrete developments concealed behind this concept. A few core points will therefore be summarized here which form the background of the discussion on global governance.

Globalization: is the world still governable?

The significance and scope of globalization continue to be a matter of dispute. Some authors regard globalization as no more than a myth or an interest-driven, put-up-or-shut-up argument in the debate on locational policy and practice; others see in it a secular mega-trend and the most momentous socioeconomic and technological structural upheaval since the onset of the industrial revolution. But the one fact that is undisputed is that there is an increase and an intensification of transboundary interactions to be observed that are tying all states and societies into a network of interdependencies, at the same time exposing them, with their different degrees of vulnerability, to international development trends.

Globalization is here a synonym of interdependence. To emphasize their multidimensionality and their deep effects, Willy Brandt often spoke of the 'interdependence of interdependencies.' *Global Trends*, brought out by the Development and Peace Foundation, documents these interdependencies. The new quality of globalization is, however, to be sought not only in the intensification of the interdependencies and mutual vulnerabilities between states, it also finds expression in an erosion of internal sovereignty, that is, in a narrowing down of the scopes of action open to governments.

The dispute on whether the spheres of interdependencies and transnational interactions, growing as they are like a web or tissue in scope and density, might be more aptly termed internationalization than globalization is more or less sophistical in character. But there is a large measure of agreement on the trends, dimensions, and impacts of the developments in world society, world economy, and world politics referred to here, whatever they might be called elsewhere, as globalization:

1. Far from representing something entirely new, globalization is the acceleration of the 'Europeanization of the world,' which was set in train centuries ago; it is not an ominous natural occurrence, either, but the result of politically informed deregulation strategies. We would be wasting our time demonizing it, because it is impossible to opt out of the development trends of world history; but we are urgently called upon to control its inherent dynamics politically and to breathe new life into the formative powers of politics. Today the question is how, in increasingly unbounded spaces, nation-states are to preserve their ability to shape politics and resolve problems.

2. Globalization offers both risks and opportunities; it has winners and losers, at the level of states and within societies in all regions of the world. On the one hand, it benefits the technologically superior 'OECD world' and offers competitive NICs possibilities in a world market deregulated by the World Trade Organization (WTO), while on the other, it threatens to marginalize further entire regions in economic and political terms. The 1999 *Human Development Report* provides data that substantiate this tendency,

which consists of an unequal and therefore conflict-laden distribution of the costs and benefits of globalization. Such polarization tendencies run directly counter to the construct of 'One World.'

3. Like a world court, the world market sits in judgment on the competitiveness and with it the development chances of nations. Under the increasingly rigorous conditions of international competition, social and environmental standards are everywhere, even in the OECD countries, coming under intense pressure. An increasingly deregulated free trade is increasing the temptation to secure competitive advantages at the expense of man and nature. In its *Limits to Competition* (1996) the Group of Lisbon noted: 'If the principle of competition is not curbed through regulatory policy, the outcome will be a victory for the social-Darwinist principle of the survival of the fittest, which knows nothing of social and ecological boundaries.' Human rights organizations are pointing to the danger that globalization could undermine already achieved human rights standards.

4. The question of the manageability of world problems, to which, in the 'global risk society' (Ulrich Beck), no state can turn a blind eye, has become the central problem of world politics. The globalization of the economy and technology, of communications and transportation systems also entails an internationalization of negative, undesirable developments. In an interdependent world insular thinking is tantamount to a loss of reality and a refusal to take cognizance of the multilevel interdependencies facing us. Problems in seemingly remote regions – immiseration, environmental degradation, poverty-related migration, or wars – have global boomerang effects.

In his report to the Club of Rome, Yehezkel Dror (1994) raised the skeptical question: 'Is the earth still governable?' His answer: Not by conventional means. As the gap continues to widen between the globalization of world problems and the abilities of the world's states to deal with them using conventional methods and instruments of national power and interest politics, the political sphere is going to have to take new approaches in domestic and foreign policy if it is to avoid the pitfalls left by its own powerlessness.

If problems are globalized, politics has no choice but to follow. In this case a sporadic and reactive crisis management is no longer sufficient, and what we need instead is new regulative or organizational structures. If the world is still to be governable in the twenty-first century, it will have to be governed differently from the way it was in the twentieth century. Two decades ago Willy Brandt emphasized in his introduction to the *Brandt Report* (1980):

> Whether we like it or not: we are faced with more and more problems that concern humanity as a whole, and consequently their solutions will also have to be increasingly internationalized. The globalization of risks and challenges – war, chaos, self-destruction – calls for a species of 'world domestic policy' that extends far beyond the horizon of parish-pump politics, but also beyond national boundaries.

The attempt to find responses to the challenges of globalization is referred to by some as global policy or world domestic policy, by others as world regulatory policy or global structural policy, and by many more as global governance, a term introduced to the international discussion by the Commission on Global Governance. But this term is also associated with a number of different notions.

The journal *Global Governance*, the brainchild of the United Nations University (UNU), equates the term with more multilateralism, that is, with an intensification of international cooperation in international organizations and regimes. Its subtitle alone points to this understanding of the matter: *A Review of Multilateralism and International Organizations*. The UN system here constitutes the navel of both the world and of global governance. While the 1995 report of the Commission on Global Governance did place reform of the UN system and the UN Charter in the center of its strategic thinking, the report, under its landmark title *Our Global Neighbourhood*, in some areas broke entirely new ground: the concern here is not only to come up with a concept of global politics by upgrading the UN system, but to devise at the same time a new model of politics which contains the seeds of altered roles for the spheres of state, economy, and society.

Building blocks of a global governance architecture

In the discussion on the chances of shaping the process of globalization, organizing world peace, and coming to terms with word problems, there is a small group of 'globalists' who cling to the vision of a world state. The central credo of the 'world federalists' is that 'durable peace presupposes a world order in which state sovereignty is restricted to such an extent that an executive authority of an order higher than national governments would be in a position to enforce global legal norms against individuals and groups' (Brauer 1995: 217). This somewhat hedged plea for a world state is not shared by the architects of global governance.

1. Global governance and global government (the latter term meant in the sense of world government or world state) are two different things. Global government is neither a realistic nor a desirable option in that any such bureaucratic super-authority would be more than hard-pressed to win democratic legitimation and would at the same time be far removed from the actual problems to be solved. Worldwide, decentralization is on the agenda of political reform. The pressure of globalization is encouraging a new and positive look at regional organizations as alliances geared to protection and resistance; these mobilize at the national and local levels an awareness of the need for scopes of autonomous action. A 'world King Kong' in the form of a world state would do little more than intensify all of the well-known ills of centralism and bureaucratism. The vision of global governance is more in keeping with Kant's world federation of free republics with a necessary minimum of centralism. Kant's justification of why sovereign states should embark upon a federation of this sort remains valid: the 'need' to maintain scopes for political action. One consideration that retains its validity for today's discourse on global governance is the imperative of 'republicanism', i.e. democracy and the rule of law, set out by Kant.

2. Global governance rests on different forms and levels of international coordination, cooperation, and collective decision-making, with international organizations taking on these coordination functions and contributing to the development of global modes of perception. Regimes are used to translate the will to cooperation into internationally binding rules. In such regimes states enter into agreements governing the way in which common problems are dealt with. The former are rightly termed core elements of *'governance without government'* (see Rosenau and Czempiel 1992). Even hegemons are willing to accept such regimes because they regulate states of affairs that promote their own well-being and which they are unable to regulate on their own.

3. The constraint to cooperate leads states to renounce some of their sovereignty, an effect which globalization and interdependence structures have long since had in any case. If they are to show themselves to be capable of cooperation, even the major powers are going to have to accept 'shared sovereignties', which, as the example of the EU shows, need not mean losses at all, but may just as well entail gains in common scopes of action and problem-solving capacities. Thanks to global governance the classic understanding of sovereignty, which has in any case been diminished by the increasing permeability of the boundaries dividing the world's states from one another, is finally becoming an anachronistic relic of the billiard-ball model of international relations and has been supplanted by a model constructed on the image of the web or tissue.

4. The ongoing realignment of the weights of world politics and the world economy – often referred to as the 'multipolar world' – has been accompanied by a process of regionalization, which has in turn been intensified by the pressure of globalization. The concurrence of globalization and regionalization and globalization and localization ('glocalization') is one of the structure-building development trends of world society and world politics. In all regions we can observe the formation of more or less successful zones of cooperation and integration, with the EU constituting the most highly developed model of regional governance. Global governance must build on such regional cores of cooperation, utilizing them as an organizational foundation, since the principle of subsidiarity remains a prudent option in the global context and can prevent the development of costly but inefficient and inflated centers of bureaucratism.

Global governance is not a project involving only governments or international organizations as instruments of the world's states. What is new about the conception advanced by the Commission on Global Governance, the one that distinguishes it from all others, is that it calls not only for more state-organized multilateralism but also for 'cooperation of governmental and nongovernmental actors from the local to the global level.' This public/private partnership in horizontally and vertically networked structures refers not only to the growing importance of globally operating 'multis' and media corporations that control global telecommunications, it at the same time points to the increasingly transnational character of non-governmental organizations (NGOs). They have long since been an important element of the dramaturgy of world conferences and have now, in several 'soft' policy areas (environment, human rights, development), gained an influential voice in shaping policy, on top of their consultative and corrective functions.

Nation-states can no longer, as they did at the Vienna Congress, simply do as they please in a world of diplomatic exclusivity. This is what UN Secretary-General Kofi Annan meant when he spoke (in 1999) of a 'quiet revolution' behind the stage of the world of states. The initiative taken by worldwide NGO campaigns in bringing about the convention on landmines as well as the effective influence exerted by NGOs on national and international environmental and human rights policies have raised the question whether an 'NGOization of world politics' has already taken place. Notwithstanding the occasional overestimation of their capacities, the role played by NGOs in the future is likely be somewhat less comprehensive. But in various policy areas they not only inject into the international system considerable potentials for dealing effectively with problems, they also make use of forms of transnational action toward the end of organizing a 'counter-hegemonic globalization.'

Nation-states, with their capacity to take authoritative decisions unilaterally, continue to be the main actors of international politics, and they constitute the chief pillars on which any global governance architecture will rest. The latter is, however, no longer viable without network-like interlinkages between the state and the spheres of economy and society. Public/private partnership means that the state, in cooperation with social groups, is called on to work out joint solutions to common problems. Participatory, bottom-up decision-making procedures have long since proven to be more efficient than centralist top-down procedures.

Presuppositions of global governance

The Commission on Global Governance underlined three presuppositions that must be given if global governance is to work and which Kant pointed to in his defining article on 'Perpetual Peace.' First, any peace secured for the long term can come about only in and between states constituted under the rule of law ('republican' states). Second, while a peace-oriented world politics is not in need of a world state, it is reliant on the regulative force of an international law valid and binding within a federation of free republics.

Third, the emerging world society must build on a 'cosmopolitan constitution' with 'world civil rights,' on a foundation of universal human rights.

1. Global governance, or a world regulative policy, can be effected only by invigorating the rule of law at the global level. The rule of law means good governance at home (accountability of those responsible for government, an independent judiciary, respect for human rights), and the rule of international law in international relations. Here we run up against the problematic that global governance is overburdened when called upon not only to restore the monopoly of state power where terror or anarchy rules, but to create democratic conditions as well. In principle, however, global governance is bound up with a 'culture of legitimate intervention' that refuses to remain idle when anywhere in the world – be it in Rwanda, Kosovo, or East Timor – severe human rights violations are being perpetrated.

2. The establishment of the International Criminal Court was an important step on the way to civilizing international relations, even though – of all countries – the leading world powers (the US, Russia, China) have refused to sign the convention. The arrest of General Pinochet by the British police on the warrant of a Spanish judge was a signal that dictators indicted for grave violations of human rights will no longer be able to feel safe in countries ruled by law. The design of the International Court of Justice in The Hague as the 'cathedral of international law' is, however, impaired by the serious flaw that it permits states to ignore its decisions without having to fear sanctions. It must be said that for this reason as well the term 'world domestic policy,' which would presuppose a supranational authority capable of imposing sanctions, is a problematical one.

3. The development of an international culture of cooperation presupposes, aside from universally accepted rules, including procedural rules in bargaining systems, a foundation consisting of shared values and principles of action as well as a minimum of trust, reliability, willingness to compromise, and respect for the legitimate interests of others. Binding rule systems are the *sine qua non* of any sort of order, be it at the national or the international level.

As is shown by the dispute over the universality of human rights and the demands that they be culturally relativized as 'Asian values' or 'Islamic values,' cultural conflicts are making it difficult to build the minimum consensus present in latent form in the conventions on human rights. While the political scientist Samuel Huntington (1996), in his scenario of a 'clash of civilizations,' dismisses the principle of universality as a legal fiction, the theologian Hans Küng (1997) places all his hope on the chance that an intercultural dialogue will prove able to come up with a 'world ethics.' The intention of the one is to use dialogue to prevent what the other would, if need be, respond to by force of arms, overlooking in the process the actual causes of conflicts, which revolve around questions of distribution and power, and draping them in the cloak of cultural conflicts.

What speaks for Küng's option is the assumption that in the future intercultural dialogue will have a confidence-building and peace-keeping function that is similar in importance to the role played by arms control at an earlier juncture. This intercultural dialogue will, however, have to abandon the one-way street of North–South relations and aim to develop a 'common culture of learning.' Western societies will have to stop seeing themselves as and acting like organizations whose job is to instruct and correct others and endeavor to develop into societies with a penchant for learning.

Küng's plea for a global ethics of responsibility is more than the moral appeal of a theologian: without an ethics that takes on respon-sibility for 'common survival' – as the matter is put in the *Brandt Report* – global governance will not get off the ground. This is what is meant when people speak, with a certain measure of pathos, of a 'community of fate and responsibility.' Traditional concepts of social ethics such as equity and solidarity are acquiring a global frame of reference. There is thus broad general agreement on the normative structural principles of global governance, although experience shows that it will be a long way from consensus on principles to action on the basis of these principles. Here power-backed hegemony often reigns supreme over the romanticism of an international culture of cooperation. Global governance is a target projection, not a description of the actual state of the international system.

Contradictions between insights and action

True, the actors of world politics have increasingly begun to embrace the insight that globalization goes beyond the problem-solving capacities of nation-states and that the international crisis management mechanisms presently in use – be it within the framework of the G7/G8 or the UN Security Council – are no longer adequate to the new tasks beginning to emerge. The pressure of problems has forced this insight on us. But thus far the result has been no more than a dilatory muddling through, the result of which is a reactive ad hoc crisis management that works mainly when the interests of a limited number of states are at stake.

The nation-states – above all the leading world powers – are still acting as though they were able to solve today's and tomorrow's world problems with the aid of the nation-based policy models of yesterday. The 'sacred cow' of a sovereignty, long since anachronistic, and a mindset in the traditional categories of national power and interest policies constitute daunting hurdles on the way to the global thinking and action that Willy Brandt so emphatically called for twenty years ago. There exist great doubts as to whether the project of global governance will be able to keep the promises that its architects have projected into it.

On the threshold to a new century we have not, as we had hoped after the end of the Cold War, come any closer to a 'new world order,' but are instead experiencing relapses into a 'world disorder' only partially regulated by international rules, one that for many analysts of world events recalls the 'world of yesterday.' Dieter Senghaas (1994) posed the oracular question: 'Where is the world headed for?' This drift can be illustrated with reference to many examples:

- Under the growing pressure generated by transboundary problems and the consequent need for stepped-up international cooperation, the latter part of the twentieth century may well have earned the latter the title of the 'century of international organizations and regimes.' However, these instruments of cooperative action, with the possible exception of the international financial and trade organizations (IMF, World Bank, WTO), which have been equipped with power and capital by the OECD countries, cannot yet be seen as agents endowed with the capacity to act. We have instead experienced a crisis of multilateralism stemming from the circumstance that the superpower US has seen fit to follow the maxim: As much unilateralism as possible, as much multilateralism as absolutely necessary. True, we now have in the World Trade Organization

(WTO) a comprehensive trade regime, but we still lack the social and ecological safeguards that could set limits to both the exploitation of man and nature as well as to 'predatory capitalism' (Helmut Schmidt), the international competitive regime that could ensure that such behavior is not rewarded in international competition, and the international monetary regime that could curb speculative 'casino capitalism.' But the pressure of problems – such as the Asia crisis and the dumping practices associated with low social and environmental standards – has provided a situation in which these issues have been put on the agenda of new international bargaining rounds.

- While we have in *Agenda 21*, adopted in 1992 at the Rio Conference, a comprehensive action program for dealing with global environmental problems, we have experienced at the follow-up conferences an embarrassing haggling on the part of the signatories aimed at weakening as far as possible, at the behest of powerful interest groups, as many as possible of the binding rules designed to reduce environmental burdens. In global environmental policy we have experienced much gradualistic progress, while at the same time seeing only tottering steps in climate policy.

- The 1995 Copenhagen World Social Summit solemnly declared 'war on poverty,' and in 1996 the OECD countries, proposing an international strategy for development, subscribed to the objective of using targeted investments in basic social services as a vehicle for cutting by half the number of poor people in the world by the year 2015. At the same time, however, these very countries have cut their development budgets and moved further and further away from the voluntary commitments signed in Copenhagen. Less money, however, will mean that the great problems of the present and future will continue to elude solution.

- The other world conferences have also adopted landmark action programs aimed at solving the most pressing world problems such as population and food. Implementation of these programs could defuse some disaster scenarios, but no progress is being made here thanks to a lack of willingness to draw the right conclusions from existing insights and fine-sounding declarations of intent. Nor have fears of a 'population explosion' or a new and unparalleled wave of mass migration, which are already being dramatized as security problems, proven able to prevent cuts in the funding available for the UN Population Fund (UNFPA).

The jargon of development policy nowadays avoids the term Third World, preferring instead to fit the latter into a frame defined as 'One World.' Social ethics has long since internationalized the norms of equity and solidarity. At the same time we have observed that the 'poor world' was being slowly but surely decoupled from this 'One World.' The world economic triad (North America–EU–East Asia) is of course also the hub of this world.

- The world has not become any more peaceful since the end of the Cold War. In his *Agenda for Peace*, former UN Secretary-General Boutros Boutros-Ghali presented concrete proposals for preventing and managing conflicts. Think tanks specialized in security and peace have operationalized these proposals. The international community, however, has as a rule responded either not at all or too late when warlike conflicts have taken shape anywhere in the world. NATO intervened in Kosovo without any mandate from the UN Security Council, endowing itself with a justification for further interventions in the future, but without taking the trouble to work out an intervention regime acceptable under international law, which would be needed if a global 'culture of legitimate intervention' is to develop.

Do these observations, after all, not permit the conclusion that the loud calls for global governance are unable to prevent a 'global struggle of all against all'? Yet it is also possible to draw an entirely different conclusion, the one that constitutes the argumentational foundation of the present contribution. If we are to avoid this threatening Hobbesean scenario, we must rely on global governance. Because the world's states are unable to solve world problems with the aid of conventional methods and instruments, because globalization is overpowering the governance capacities of nation-states, with even world powers forced to rely on international cooperation to secure their own future, it is essential to set a new course for world politics.

Such insights have long since been up for discussion, and not only in academic think tanks, circles of professing 'globalists,' and the planning staffs of foreign ministries. There is also a great variety of approaches to global governance in various policy areas. In addressing the question whether the glass of global governance is half full or half empty, Ingvar Carlsson, the co-chairman of the Commission on Global Governance, notes that there are already so many positive developments that the question appears to be more a rhetorical one. But these selective forms of global governance are not adequate to the challenges posed by the most pressing problems of the future.

Global governance, development, and peace

There now exist several global models that concur on central points with the proposals of the Commission on Global Governance. Many of these proposals had already been addressed in the *Brandt Report*, which so resolutely placed its stakes on multilateral solutions that it was consigned – particularly in Washington and London – to the wastepaper basket of banned regulatory policy literature of Thatcherism and Reaganism. Their brand of neoliberal orthodoxy included stalwart resistance to any approaches based on global governance, and above all to any positive assessment of international organizations, burgeoning international bureaucracies, and the establishment of multilateral development funds.

The 'Group of Lisbon': justifications for global governance grounded in contract theory

A report presented by the Group of Lisbon (1996), which has brought together mainly social-democratic intellectuals under the initiative of Ricardo Petrella, was received with considerable public resonance. This group too justified its 'global approach' with an eye to the need to adapt world politics to the conditions of globalization, noting that the task of formulating and shaping world politics places nation-states before formidable difficulties. If they are to overcome the insidious powerlessness with which world politics is afflicted, institutions and rules of political governance will have to be put in place at the level at which the global players of the world economy operate.

   To rein in the destructive potential of the market mechanism, the Group proposed, first, a 'system of cooperative global governance' in which international civil society as well as enlightened elites would be involved and, second, four global agreements under the umbrella of a 'global treaty' borrowing from classical contract theory:

- a *basic needs pact* aimed at overcoming mass poverty in the world;
- a *culture pact* aimed at promoting intercultural dialogue between cultures and religions;
- a *democracy pact* aimed at involvement of civil society in co-operative global governance, democratization of the UN system, and convocation of a 'global citizen's assembly' (i.e. geared to realizing ideas propagated as well by Jürgen Habermas or Johan Galtung);
- an *earth pact* on the model of *Agenda 21*.

The question is what progress these proposed pacts might mean vis-à-vis agreements already concluded or action programs agreed upon by UN world conferences, if, that is to say, we disregard the constructive idea of a global social contract. A basic needs pact is already contained in the legally binding 'social pact'; an earth pact is part of Agenda 21 as well as various other environmental conventions; a culture pact is anchored in numerous UNESCO resolutions and programs, even though some of these are more binding than others.

The democracy pact has the least chance of realization, the main problem being its proposal of convoking a 'global citizen's assembly' with an eye to democratizing the UN system. Who is supposed to be represented in it? How are representatives to be elected? How are the seats to be distributed? What rights are delegates to have? The 'right to democracy,' which was decided on in 1999 by the UN Human Rights Commission and whose core elements are already anchored in the catalogues of human rights, is unlikely to engender any worldwide effects. On the other hand, the idea of a democracy pact recalls a core problem of multilateralism that has only partially been solved in the EU. How are decisions to be legitimated that have been removed from the sphere of competence of nation states and shifted to the multilateral level?

The great work of the philosopher Otfried Höffe (1999) on 'Democracy in the Age of Globalization' holds out the promise of a comprehensive answer to the question how democracy could and should be organized in a 'subsidiary and federal world republic.' But his answer also consists of a number of cautious intermediate steps which he clothes in a simile (p. 427):

The establishment of a democratic world order must be undertaken even more cautiously than the refitting of a ship at high sea: just as the ship must remain seaworthy, world society must never endanger its state of peace and lawfulness, as relative as the latter may be; on the contrary, it should enhance its seaworthiness, i.e. improve the measure of democracy and the rule of law that has already been achieved ... As a means of gathering experience and avoiding any erosion of qualified democracy it would be best to start out with a confederated world republic before moving to a federal world republic.

In other words, instead of reaching for the stars of a 'global democracy' it would be better to expand democracy in the framework of the national elements of a 'confederated world republic.' There is, first and foremost, no better solution than effective control of the actions of states in international organizations by parliaments and the public sphere, which often derive their information from knowledgeable and increasingly transnationally networked NGOs. The latters' strength lies in their watchdog function.

True, there are large areas of agreement between the global governance architecture of the Commission on Global Governance, the 'system of cooperative global governance' propagated by the Group of Lisbon, and Höffe's plea for a 'subsidiary and federal world republic,' but the arguments adduced in the present volume in favor of global governance are more concrete and at the same time more realistic in that they take into account not only what is desirable but also what is feasible, and they are in part highly skeptical toward the chances and the effects of international rules.

Rules for sustainable development and peace

Even among *laissez-faire* prophets of a Smithian stamp it is undisputed that markets are in need of a regulative framework in order to be able to unfold their productive forces. Without any regulatory policy competition tends to culminate in social and ecological dumping. This is just as true for national economies as it is for the globalizing economy – the difference being that there already are national regulatory rules, while as yet such rules exist only in a rudimentary stage of development at the international level, if we except here the integration project that is the EU, which can be seen as a laboratory of regional governance.

What is true for the world economy can be generalized for other policy areas. The 1999 *Human Development Report* warned that the forces of the market would not correct the imbalances in the world:

what is required to secure the benefits of globalization for the well-being of people and not for profit, the authors note, is more political governance. The objective is to find a global regulative framework in five policy areas that represent pillars of a new world order and must be interlinked if they are to be viable and sustainable: a world financial and trade regime, a world social and environmental regime, and a world peace regime.

Reconstruction of the international financial architecture

The *Brandt Report* identified the disorder in the international financial system as one of the key problems of the world economy and called on the IMF to stabilize exchange rates. This demand for institutional regulation went completely unheard in the heyday of neoliberalism, especially since in the 1980s the IMF, the world's financial policeman, had its hands full managing the international debt crisis. And the activity stemming from international financial policy was not preventive but ad hoc-reactive. It was again the pressure of problems and the particular vulnerability of western investors that, following the Mexico crisis of 1994/95 and the Asia crisis of 1997/98, impelled the G7 to think more intensively about regulating the international financial markets. Fears inspired by the writing on the wall suggesting that a new large-scale world economic crisis was in the offing lent wings to this reflection. Now not only weighty financial organizations like the IMF and the Bank for International Settlements (BIS) saw a need for regulation, but even a speculator of the caliber of George Soros (1998) was warning of the self-destructive tendencies of speculative 'casino capitalism.'

Under this problem-related pressure the Cologne G7/G8 Summit, held in the summer of 1999, adopted a statement of intent on building a new international financial architecture. But it is still in dispute what shape the latter should be given and what role the IMF should play in it. Many experts (including bankers) are in favor of strengthening banking supervision, more transparency of financial markets, and more responsibility of private banks in tackling financial crises, but are against all proposals aimed at more strongly regulating the international financial markets by establishing a supranational standing committee for global regulation. Consequently, they see a Tobin Tax on speculative transactions, favored by UNDP and many NGOs, not only as hardly practicable at the global level but also as harmful to trade and investment.

Nevertheless, a Tobin Tax or similar attempts to bring 'casino capitalism' under control remain on the agenda. The World Bank even recently rediscovered it as a possible source of financing for multilateral environmental and development funds – once the donor countries had begun cutting the multilateral shares of their development budgets. The need for money to finance multilateralism could help overcome objections rooted in technical market-related policy considerations. At the latest, the next major financial crisis that also endangers the well-being of western creditors will lend strength to the call on the world of finance for a new world financial order. The self-healing forces of the market will prove unable to cope with the problems of a completely over-indebted world and the crisis proneness of financial markets. Even over the medium term a renovation of the derelict Bretton Woods structures engineered in 1944 will no longer suffice, and they will have to be wholly revamped or rebuilt from scratch.

For the great majority of developing countries the term 'new international financial architecture' means above all comprehensive and sustainable debt relief. The IMF and G7, Paris Club and London Club were quite successful in the 1980s in managing acute debt crises, though they continually deferred the need to come up with a durable solution – with the consequence that the mountain of debt has continued to grow. True, the 1999 Cologne Summit promised the insolvent poorest developing countries (the so-called HIPCs) relief from their intolerably high debt burden, but without tying the foreign debt of the other developing countries and NICs, which is far higher in quantitative terms, into the problem of designing a 'new international financial architecture.' So, in this core area of North–South relations, ad hoc crisis management remains the rule, a fact that we might refer to as sober and pragmatic, but also a fact that, from a different perspective, must be seen as lacking in sustainability.

The causes of the debt crisis are both homemade and exogenous. There is an old dispute as to whether the main causes are faulty developments (such as mismanagement, waste, corruption, capital flight, military spending, etc.) or, as the debtor countries and their interest organizations tend to emphasize, world-economic factors. The core thesis of the 1999 Annual Report of the UN Conference on Trade and Development (UNCTAD), that international trade relations present obstacles to any way out of the debt trap, is, however, unlikely to arouse much controversy. This is why the calls voiced by the Group of 77 and the group of nonaligned countries for a 'more equitable world trade regime' have remained at the center of all North–South talks.

World trade regime: the regulatory policy dispute over the WTO

For most developing countries trade relations are of existential significance. From the first world trade conferences and GATT rounds to the WTO's 'Millenium Round' these countries have demanded a 'new international economic order' which would guarantee them higher and more stable raw materials prices, better market access via reductions of tariff and non-tariff trade barriers, and better terms of trade. The rules on which the WTO is based have given rise to a comprehensive, effective, and highly powerful world trade regime that covers the trade in goods and services and includes protection for intellectual property rights.

There are a number of factors in these international trade liberalization rules that deserve to be criticized. First, the industrialized countries have used their greater power to secure many advantages for themselves, particularly as regards goods in which developing countries would have competitive advantages. Second, inadequate consideration is accorded to the protection-worthy interests of countries weaker in terms of competitiveness. Third, the exclusion of social and ecological criteria, on which, in turn, the developing countries insist with a view to avoid being forced to give up the comparative advantages that accrue to them from lower social and environmental standards. A world trade regime must prevent any beggar-thy-neighbor policy, any devaluation races, protectionism, or social and environmental dumping that seeks to solve national problems at the expense of trade partners, and it must be in accord with the norms of international law. Exploitation of children or women in 'world market factories' not only contravenes the child labor convention or the social standards established by the ILO, at the same time it distorts competition (e.g. in the labor-intensive textile and footwear industries).

It is not only the politically correct environmental and development organizations but also the European Parliament as well as some individual states, above all the Nordic countries, that are calling for social and ecological improvements in the WTO rules, because they perceive a goal conflict between the WTO's principles of free trade and the imperatives of sustainable development.

The developing countries view this debate in the North with great suspicion. What they expect of a world trade regime is not social and ecological principles but the establishment of conditions ensuring fair trade, the reduction of protectionism (above all the agricultural protectionism of the EU), a greater share in the trade profits that are accruing to the beneficiaries of the WTO, and, not least, more influence in the WTO, in which they tend to see – as in the case of IMF and World Bank – instruments of western interests. What architects of the WTO promised – not only to Subsaharan Africa but to all other groups of countries – was welfare gains through free trade. In other words, they have been unable to buy off the weaker participants in the world economy with the formula 'trade not aid,' and they also had no choice but to console the latter with prospects of more development aid, which then failed to materialize.

In view of the growing economization of international relations, and in the wake of the increasing competitive pressure arising in connection with the WTO's rules, trade policy has become an important issue to all countries, but one that has existential implications for developing countries, and for this reason a world trade regime must bring about a fair composition of interests, one that provides welfare gains that are not restricted to the world's most competitive trading nations. Fair trade must not only embrace the fairly traded coffee, tea, and honey sold in 'One World' shops, it should become the guiding principle of a world trade regime that is concerned not only with trade liberalization, but is at the same time devoted to ecologizing and humanizing the world economy. This is why the WTO's trade regime needs to be revised.

From a world social regime to the 'new development architecture'

The call for a world social regime may in some ways recall the Group of Lisbon's demand for a basic needs pact. But what this implies is not only provision for the basic needs of the world's population, but the realization of the human rights codified in the 'Social Pact,' the ILO standards, which are also binding under international law, and the protective rights of children codified in the Convention on Children.

The goal of a world social regime first of all requires every individual state to create the conditions that ensure a decent existence for its citizens by building a domestic social system. But this cannot be accomplished without solidary efforts on the part of other states and societies and presupposes that global corporations will comply with internationally agreed social and environmental standards that are designed to curb 'predatory capitalism.' UN Secretary-General Kofi Annan has proposed a human rights and environment pact between the UN and the private sector as a means of humanizing the world market:

> Many enterprises are big investors, important employers, and leading producers in dozens of countries throughout the world. This power entails great chances but also great responsibility. Human rights and adequate labor and environmental standards can be promoted by the management of individual factories ... Why should not industry provide a good example and ensure that human rights are supported and respected in their own corporate practice and that human rights violations are not encouraged?

A global ethic of responsibility or a 'global neighborhood' would entail a commitment to global solidarity and burden-sharing between the winners and losers of globalization. A development policy conceived as global structural policy would have to seek to contribute to improving the political, legal, social, and ecological framework at the national and international levels, to reduce the global welfare gap – a contributory cause of a good number of conflicts – and to promote the development of social and political structures that would make it possible to imbue social human rights with life. These rights do, of course, have to be fought for and won by societies themselves. But it is possible to provide external support for the 'empowerment' of the forces of civil society. This is a task both for official development assistance, with its newfound pro-grammatic commitment to promoting democracy, and for the 'International' of the forces of civil society.

The action program adopted by consensus at the Copenhagen World Social Summit of 1995 includes a timetable for the creation of a world social order that imposes obligations on industrial and developing countries alike, as well as on governments, industry, and society. Without the financial, organizational, and technological potentials of multinational corporations, without the expertise provided by the sciences, and without the consultative and monitoring functions of NGOs, states and international organizations will themselves not succeed in coming to terms with world problems.

Recently, and entirely in the sense of global governance, the World Bank called for a 'new development architecture' (the so-called Comprehensive Development Framework), and it is seeking to create a global development network to forge 'coalitions for change.' The 54th annual assembly of IMF and World Bank in the fall of 1999 reached agreement not only on the funding of the debt relief initiative for HIPCs decided on at the Cologne G7 Summit, but also called on the IMF to orient its future structural adjustment programs more markedly to the goals of poverty reduction and to replace its 'Extended Structural Adjustment Facility' (ESAF) with a 'Poverty Reduction and Growth Facility.' It is reform initiatives like these that the pressure of problems sometimes engenders.

The concern is not simply more development aid, which in any case is not going to materialize, but to work out in development finance new forms of public/private partnerships. There is no lack of awareness of what has to be done or of the resources needed to effectively fight poverty; what is lacking is the political will, as Willy Brandt noted in his Introduction to the *Brandt Report*:

> Never has mankind had such a diversity of technical and financial resources to deal with hunger and poverty. The enormous task can be mastered if the necessary common will is mobilized.

It is not only that many environmental problems are the result of mass poverty, but population growth, painted in the frightening hues of a 'P-bomb', is highest where poverty is greatest (as, for instance, in Subsaharan Africa). At the same time, population development in some regions has confirmed the prescription of the 1994 Cairo World Population Conference. Wherever targeted investments have been made in educational and health systems, birth and fertility rates have declined at surprisingly rapid rates. Poverty reduction – or the realization of basic human rights – is, in other words, the *conditio sine qua non* for any deceleration of population growth and thus at the same time for peaceful and sustainable development, because more people mean more consumption of nature and more conflicts over increasingly scarce resources.

International development policy has meanwhile also recognized that women should play a key role not only in family planning, but also in all subsistence-related areas. Without the liberation of women from exploitation and repression at home and in society as a whole, and without the political emancipation of women, a world social order would remain a distorted patriarchalist fantasy. This is why the UNDP's *Human Development Report* features both a Gender-related Index (GDI) and a Gender Empowerment Measure (GEM).

World environmental regime: the project of a world organization for environment and development

The model of 'sustainable development,' which was introduced into the international discussion by the 1987 *Brundtland Report* and took on the shape of a model for socially and environmentally sound global development when it went into the making of Agenda 21, adopted by the 1992 Rio Conference, has for two reasons proven to be particularly innovative. First, it left the established one-way street of North–South relations by raising questions and demands bearing on the industrial countries' structural capacity to change and adapt to the future. The question was now: How is the North to develop? The model of sustainability would prove credible only if, for instance, the US or UK were to focus not only on environmental protection as a priority of their own development policy, but also advance the cause of an ecological restructuring of their own economies. Second, the *Local Agenda 21* set in train an unprecedented discussion and learning process which was an example for cooperation between governmental and nongovernmental actors at all levels of action and in which the Commission on Global Governance saw the constitutive principle of global governance.

Although the greatest advances made thus far have been in the field of global environmental policy – because even the global players were threatened by ecological crises – the model of sustainability, already inflated into a catchword, is hobbled by deficits in implementation at all levels of action. The environmental regimes are a classic example of the selective manner in which world problems are processed. How could we more effectively organize global environmental policy, while at the same time avoiding the danger that the systemic linkage between environment and development, rooted in the model of 'sustainable development,' could be dissolved by a fragmentation of institutions and competences in the UN system?

Udo Ernst Simonis and Frank Biermann (1998) are working on the architecture for a World Environment and Development Organization which promises to meet both these conditions while at the same time creating the institutional conditions required for a comprehensive and efficient world environmental regime. The obvious objection is that the plan to create a super-agency would, in the first place, provoke the resistance of many countries that fear any environmental interventionism and that, in the second place, the UN bureaucracies – UNDP and UNEP, set to be merged here, might serve as an example of this – have not exactly stood out when called upon to act.

What would be just as important as the final institutional framework of a functioning world environmental regime is, first, a credible partnership between industrialized countries, NICs, and developing countries, in that important global policy goals (such as CO_2 reduction, protection of rainforests and biodiversity, sustainable exploitation of fish stocks) cannot be realized against the will of reluctant country majorities. Second, more participation of environmental groups in advisory bodies at different levels, because the former now have a high level of expert knowledge and articulate the interests of concerned population groups. The Commission on Sustainable Development set a good example by institutionalizing a 'multi-stakeholder dialogue' which can serve to involve civil society actors in the shaping of global environmental policy.

The Simonis and Biermann proposal is, for the foreseeable future, just as doomed to failure as is the call of the 'world federalists' to convene without delay a world conference on global governance. At present things do not look good for multilateralism. This is, however, no argument against proposals aimed at advancing the cause of global governance and a world environmental regime. Science has the task of looking ahead and thinking about solutions to problems, even though these may, at present, still appear to be concrete utopias. The world is changed not by thinking in terms of the status quo but by thinking ahead in innovative and creative terms. There is no alternative to multilateralism.

World peace regime: the linkage between development and peace

In the end, all efforts aimed at building world regimes are doomed to failure if they are not embedded in a *world peace regime*. Willy Brandt was right: 'without peace it is all nothing.' While in regions afflicted with war, chaos, and destruction peace first of all means the termination of armed conflicts and the restoration of a legitimate monopoly of power, it also implies an overcoming of the structural causes of war.

The Commission on Global Governance (1995) outlined the new dimensions of security:

Protection against external aggression remains, of course, an essential objective for national governments and therefore for the international community. But that is only one of the challenges that must be met to ensure global security. Despite the growing safety of most of the world's states, people in many areas now feel more insecure than ever. The source of this is rarely the threat of attack from the outside. Other equally important security challenges arise from threats to the earth's life-support systems, extreme economic deprivation, the proliferation of conventional small arms, the terrorizing of civilian populations by domestic factions, and gross violations of human rights. These factors challenge the security of people far more than the threat of external aggression.

The *Report on the Causes of Conflict and the Promotion of Durable Peace and Sustainable Development in Africa,* presented by UN Secretary-General Kofi Annan in April 1998, gave concrete form to the demand voiced in the *Agenda for Peace* that bi- and multilateral development policy see mass poverty and environmental degradation, human-rights violations, social discrimination and political repression as causes of conflicts. There was, in other words, a large measure of agreement on the causes of conflicts and the ways and chances to prevent them.

The search for a world peace regime places the United Nations, whose *raison d'être* has always been peacekeeping, in the center of strategies aimed at securing peace. But the UN's powerlessness to come to terms with this task, for which the main actors on the Security Council must be blamed, and the crisis of multilateralism in the wake of the unilateralist hegemonic policy of the 'sole superpower,' the US, have upset the hopes of the 'globalists' that the United Nations might become the crystallization point of a world peace regime. The NATO's self-authorization to conduct an air war against Yugoslavia not only – in violation of the UN Charter – brushed aside the UN's monopoly on authorization of the use of force, it at the same time intensified skepticism toward any 'humanitarian interventionism' aimed at preventing severe violations of human rights.

On the threshold of the twenty-first century we see the UN threatened with marginalization in the field of peace policy. Multilateral impulses toward change have lost some of their force. This means that ideas aimed at a multilateral peace regime of the type advanced by the Commission on Global Governance and the *Agenda for Peace* are now running up against obstacles that will prove difficult to overcome. It is above all the hegemonic superpower US that is resisting its integration into a multilateralism marked by shared sovereignties.

Despite the weaknesses of hegemonic notions of order, with the resistance they provoke, and the limited effectiveness of a 'world domestic policy' that seeks to use the means of external intervention to create stability in conflict regions, many peace researchers nevertheless subscribe to the idea of cooperative security in a multilateral world peace regime – and do so for two reasons bound up with the idea of global governance. First, this approach looks more to the political, social, and economic conditions of a durable peace, in this way shifting the priority of politics from intervention to prevention. Second, this preventive multi-track approach involves a large number of national and international, governmental, and nongovernmental actors in the tasks of peacekeeping and peace consolidation.

The German peace researcher Tobias Debiel (2000: 464) draws the sober conclusion: 'The concern at present cannot be to devise "grand projects" for the new millennium but to strengthen the UN as the core of a system of cooperative security.' The marginalization of the UN in matters of peace is at the bottom of this disillusionment. Still, the alternative would be either decline into anarchy or acceptance of a hegemonic world police offcer neither willing nor able to intervene whenever and wherever warlike conflicts break out. Because the great majority of countries are unwilling to choose between anarchy and hegemony, they prefer to rely on cooperative conflict management via the UN – admittedly, without abandoning hope of a reform of the UN Security Council, which will have to adapt the latter's makeup and functions to the world-political conditions in existence at the beginning of the twenty-first century. One approach that might help keep the UN from being overwhelmed by the task of keeping world peace would be to foster regional security structures (such as the OAS, OSCE, OAU, or ASEAN), which are permitted under Chapter VIII of the UN Charter.

The Development Assistance Committee (DAC) of the OECD in 1997 presented its member states with its *Guidelines on Conflict, Peace and Development*, calling upon them urgently to engage in a coordinated approach in conflict situations. A report on the 'Role of Development Cooperation in Peacemaking Measures and the

Prevention and Resolution of Conflicts,' adopted in November of 1998 by the Council of Ministers, was then keyed to these DAC guidelines. The EU's Common Foreign and Security Policy (CFSP) and Europe's development policy can do more for peace than any bilateral efforts.

Perspectives of the global governance project: vision or illusion?

The project of global governance has had to face numerous objections. It is said to be an atheoretical construct that flees from a critical analysis of tough present realities into voluntarist visions of the future. It is said to ignore both the power factor and real hegemonic interests, a fact which, in view of the real power relations in world politics and the global economy, prevents it from delivering even a concrete utopia for tomorrow's world. It is said to turn a blind eye to feminist ideas, neglecting emancipatory conflict strategies and relying too heavily on cooperative public/private partnership. 'Realists' in politics and science give the project little chance of realization. What they see emerging in the wake of globalization is intensified competition, deregulation races, and trade conflicts that cannot be curbed by global governance.

At the beginning of the twenty-first century global governance is in fact still a fragile project. A move by the Clinton administration toward a policy of unilateralist hegemonism, with the attendant tendency to dismantle the UN system, the major pillar of the global governance architecture, has undermined the idea of multilateral 'cooperative security.' There is again more talk of a 'new world disorder' than of a new world order in which not power but international law and a culture of cooperation would determine the actions of states.

However, there are also developments that show global governance to be more than an illusion: the establishment of a number of regimes that are deepening and codifying international cooperation in various policy fields; the establishment of the International Criminal Court to prosecute crimes against humanity throughout the world; a 'policy of intervention' to improve human rights and develop the rule of law by means of appropriate conditionalities and promotion instruments in development policy; the development of an international civil society that refuses to leave politics up to 'the state'; the attempts undertaken by world conferences to work out cooperative solutions to the most pressing world problems. Under the pressure generated by these problems as well as by the international NGO scene, the neoliberal 'Washington consensus' is breaking down. The annual assembly of IMF and World Bank in the fall of 1999 called on the two Bretton Woods institutions to devote more of their efforts to poverty reduction.

Numerous international organizations and negotiation processes provide forums in which to practice cooperative patterns of thinking and action and engage in learning processes that can then flow back into national decision-making processes. The pressure of problems and the concomitant growing transaction costs imposed by efforts to come up solutions without cooperation will also force global players to regulate the uncontrolled dynamics inherent in globalization and impel the 'lonely superpower' to engage in international cooperation, because the latter, alone or together with NATO, will prove unable to solve the problem of the governability of the world (see Huntington 1999). There is no future for hegemonic notions of world order in a polycentric and turbulent world.

Global governance is not a romantic project aimed at a safe and tidy 'global neighborhood,' but a realistic response to the challenges of globalization and global risks. It is an evolutionary project, developing step by step. In spite of numerous blockades, at the threshold of the twenty-first century the chances for a new world order are better than they were when the United Nations was founded – and the contours of the Cold War began to emerge. The 'age of globalism' has already begun.

References

Annan, Kofi (1998) 'The Quiet Revolution,' *Global Governance*, Vol. 4(2), pp. 123–38.

Brandt Report (The Independent Commission on International Development Issues) (1980) *North–South: A Programme for Survival*, London.

Brauer, Maja (1995) *Weltföderation. Modell globaler Gesellschaftsordnung*, Frankfurt/M.

Commission on Global Governance (1995) *Our Global Neighbourhood*, Oxford.

Debiel, Tobias (2000) 'Vereinte Nationen und Weltfriedensordnung,' in Franz Nuscheler (ed.), *Entwicklung und Frieden im 21. Jahrhundert*, Bonn, pp. 446–67.

Dror, Yehezkel (1994) *The Capacity to Govern*. A Report to the Club of Rome, Barcelona.

Group of Lisbon (1996) *Limits to Competition*, Cambridge, MA.

Höffe, Otfried (1999) Demokratie im Zeitalter der Globalisierung, Munich.

Huntington, Samuel P. (1996) *The Clash of Civilizations and the Remaking of the World Order*, New York.

Huntington, Samuel P. (1999) 'The Lonely Superpower,' *Foreign Affairs*, Vol. 78(2), pp. 35–49.

Küng, Hans (1997) *Weltethos für Weltpolitik und Weltwirtschaft*, Munich.

Nuscheler, Franz (ed.) (2000) *Entwicklung und Frieden im 21. Jahrhundert*, Bonn.

Rosenau, James N. and Czempiel, Ernst-Otto (eds.) (1992) *Governance without Government*, New York.

Senghaas, Dieter (1994) *Wohin driftet die Welt?*, Frankfurt/M.

Simonis, Udo Ernst and Frank Biermann (1998) *A World Environment and Development Organization, Development and Peace Foundation*, Policy Paper 9, Bonn.

Soros, George (1998) *The Crisis of Global Capitalism*, New York.

7
Globalization and Global Governance – A Synopsis

This synopsis attempts to assemble the pieces of the puzzle presented by individual trends, the great variety of globalization processes, and *Global Trends* in such a way that an overall picture emerges. The 20 central global trends give rise to an inductively developed understanding of globalization. It becomes clear that the policy responses to the new challenges and the current state of problem-solving capacities diverge quite considerably.

A world-embracing communications infrastructure, global market processes, universal models, global science, global juridification processes, the consolidation of international regimes and transnational actor groups are all contributing to the process of building global structures. The 'epoch of the nation-state' and the international systems corresponding to it are being successively supplanted by the 'epoch of globalism,' which is witnessing the emergence of a world society. In it we find a variety of – in part overlapping – interactions, interdependencies, problem constellations, and conflict lines taking concrete shape between local, national, and global levels of action.

The process of shaping globalization is still in its early days, though elements of a global governance architecture are emerging that will profoundly transform politics, the role of nation-states, civil societies, international and supranational organizations and regimes, and different forms of democracy. National societies that are efficient and capable of learning and integration must find answers to the new challenges. In the twenty-first century nations will at the same time transform themselves into the 'provinces' of a world society without any central governmental power, and will have to learn to solve problems of a global and transboundary nature.

World Society

Global trends	The processing of problems/ global governance approaches
1. Increasing number of people living in absolute poverty, despite many improvements in social conditions in most countries of the world.	There is a consensus on strategies aimed at reducing absolute poverty. The World Social Summit worked out viable solutions that were further given form by the DAC document entitled 'Shaping the 21st Century.' Implementation of these strategies is failing due to lack of willingness to mobilize the necessary resources.
2. Deepening social disparities in and between countries owing to current tendencies and the institutional shape given to globalization.	Progress is being made in problem description, as shown by UNDP, ILO, and World Bank documents. The debate over social, economic, and labor market policies aimed at reducing social disparities under the conditions of globalization is still in its incipient phase. This is true also of the discourse on international burden-sharing between the winners and losers of globalization. The dominance of the neoliberal model is hampering efforts to integrate social aspects into global regimes (e.g. WTO, MAI). Vested interests and power asymmetries are obstructing social

articulation of globalization in and between societies.

3. Continuing growth of the world's population, but slower growth than predicted by the United Nations at the beginning of the 1990s. Highest growth figures where poverty is most oppressive, but declining wherever development is underway.

The World Population Conference in Cairo noted that investment in health and education and training systems, and a targeted promotion of women, offer the best chances to defuse the population problem. An effective link is emerging between population policy and poverty alleviation. Yet only a limited number of countries are meeting the commitments made in Cairo and at the Copenhagen summit on poverty reduction and programs geared to population policy.

4. Wars, population pressure, mass poverty, environmental degradation, and the prosperity gap between regions and continents, as they are made visible by the media, are intensifying the pressure to migrate from poverty regions. The thrust of the 'new *Völkerwanderung*' is not to be found between South and North or East and West but within the South itself.

There is a large measure of consensus that the migration problem, which is increasingly perceived as a security problem, must be defused where it comes about: what is called for are preventive measures bound up with peace and development policies. Since conflict prevention often fails and development policy can at best provide patchy support for the goal of a socially and environmentally sound development, migration pressure will continue to rise. The potential target countries are trying to counter it by means of stepped-up border controls and restrictive political asylum laws – and doing so with success.

5. The worldwide trend toward enhancing the rights and improving the educational opportunities of women have not yet led to any reduction of their discrimination in business, politics, and society.

The world conferences in Vienna, Cairo, and Peking documented a consensus on women-specific human rights and the central role of women in the development process. Global women's networks are developing ton implement these goals. Impulses of the world conferences have, however, not yet found much expression in national implementation measures.

6. The communications revolution, one of the key driving forces behind economic, political, and cultural globalization and national social upheavals, it is still in its infancy. Communication costs are declining dramatically, though barriers to access remain high.

Knowledge about the complex effects of this trend and the need for political action is unsatisfactory. What we lack is a global institutional framework, and at the same time national regulatory efforts are doomed to failure. On the other hand, globally active NGOs can make use of the new technologies for the purpose of transnational networking.

World Economy

Global trends

The processing of problems/ global governance approaches

7. Since the 1980s nearly all developing countries and countries in transformation have found integration in the world economy. While some newly industrializing countries (NICs) have started closing the gap on the OECD economies, whole regions of the world are

At the close of the century we note in World Bank, CEPAL, and OECD (but not IMF) documents an emerging consensus on viable active economic and social policies and the central role of the state in advanced developing countries and countries in trans-

practically unable to compete internationally.

formation, one that is remedying the neoliberal concepts current in the 1970s–1980s. Further needs would include a development-conducive framework at the global level (e.g. stable financial markets, free EU market access for agricultural produce, regional cooperation). How systemic competitiveness, broad employment effects, and poverty reduction are to be achieved in weaker countries under the conditions of globalization is a question that has to be answered.

8. Long-term unemployment remains a central problem in many industrialized countries, especially that induced by the declining demand for unskilled labor. The 'end of working society' is, however, not on the global agenda.

At the national level target group-specific qualification measures, adjustment of training and innovation systems to the new conditions of the world economy, flexible labor markets, and viable social security systems are – as is documented by some success stories – the key to combating unemployment. Also, the OECD countries have yet to introduce minimum social standards and take any serious steps aimed at coordinating their economic policies with a view to preventing ruinous competition.

9. The international financial markets are destabilizing the world economy. The volume and volatility of global financial flows are growing and causing

A comprehensive reregulation of the world financial markets would be called for. The Asia crisis has focused the world's problem consciousness. It

monetary and financial crises, above all in the developing countries and countries in transformation.

would be possible to control speculation, discipline creditors, and establish new currency regimes, though any measures would have to be realized by powerful political alliances against well-organized and internationally mobile capital owners.

10. The merry-go-round of international mergers is spinning faster and faster. Global processes of concentration and monopolization are leading to the formation of supranational economic spaces and diminishing the reach of national economic policy.

The largely immobile actors (employees, labor unions, governments) are forced to come to terms with highly mobile transnational corporations, a fact that has tilted the balance of social forces in favor of the mobile actors. There are as yet no globally effective rules governing competition and cartels. Worker representations should be enlarged to form corporate-level worker councils.

11. The polycentric world economy is experiencing an increase in the competition and confrontation between the great economic powers. The EU and the US are about to open a round of competition for power and economic influence in the world economy of the twenty-first century. Multilateral regimes (e.g. WTO) and regional integration projects could find themselves in contradiction to one another.

Improvement of transatlantic economic relations is the key to stabilizing the world economy and bringing it under institutional control. But conflicts of regulative policy are becoming evident between the EU and the US in the process of articulating a new world trade regime and coming up with a framework for the global financial markets. The future shape given to the EU in terms of social and economic policy and the position it assumes in the process of developing an order for the world economy will be crucial factors determining the 'face' that global capitalism will have in the twenty-first century.

World Ecology

Global trends

The processing of problems/ global governance approaches

12. Since the Industrial Revolution man-made pollutants have been increasing the concentration of greenhouse gases, which is altering the climate.

Today the association between climate change and rising concentrations of greenhouse gases is generally acknowledged. The reduction rates fixed in the Climate Convention and the Kyoto Protocol are inadequate; the discussion on effective instruments is far from over. At the national level there are as yet hardly any viable strategies for complying with the commitments undertaken in these international agreements.

13. Since 1987 the worldwide use of ozone-depleting substances has been reduced by some 85 per cent.

The factors contributing to the success of the ozone regime have included: precise targets and timetables, verification mechanisms, the non-complex structure of the problem, and industry's interest in having a set of rules. Resource transfers to developing countries and countries in transformation were used as a means of supporting their participation.

14. Growing mobility is a key factor contributing to the greenhouse effect.

The Climate Convention and the Kyoto Protocol have taken far too little account of the problem of transportation and traffic. Thus far no viable problem-solving strategies have been developed at the national level either.

15. Environmental degradation is an increasingly important factor in violent conflicts. The environmental conflict potential must be sought at the local level.

Environmental problems are coming more and more to be perceived as potential sources of conflict. At the international level some initial steps have been taken toward processing these problems (e.g., the World Bank's global water partnership). However, whether environmental conflicts are successfully processed will be decided at the local level. Some successful approaches are already in place.

16. A dynamic global environmental policy has resulted in a growing number of environmental accords. Since the UN Conference on Environment and Development in Rio the new principle of 'common but differentiated responsibilities' has been anchored in all environmental accords. In keeping with the 'polluter pays' principle, the industrialized countries will have to bear the major share of the burden of ecological structural adjustment.

In spite of the agreements already in existence, environmental degradation goes on: the implementation of many accords is being blocked by national self-interest, the power of vested economic interests, and the present lack of sanction mechanisms. Globally active NGOs as well as the private sector are gaining more and more influence on the negotiation process.

World Politics

Global trends	The processing of problems/ global governance approaches
17. If we define peace as the absence of war between states, international relations have become more peaceful. Nevertheless, the stability of the international system is jeopardized by multiple risks: internationalization of the world's many domestic conflicts, conflicts over resources (e.g. water use rights for transboundary rivers), and regional conflicts between 'new weapon states,' which also possess weapons of mass destruction. The sharply increased number of new states formed since 1945 has, on the whole, also contributed to increasing the conflict potential.	In peace research there is a large measure of consensus that the following action strategies are required for, or conducive to, the goal of keeping the international peace and civilizing international relations: juridification of international relations, increase of economic interdependencies and intensification of international cooperation, invigoration of the peacekeeping functions of a reformed UN Security Council, an additional strengthening of the security arrangements as per Chapter VIII of the UN Charter, and, finally, promotion of sustainable peace-oriented structures through democratization and extension of democratic peace zones. Progress has been made in juridifying international relations, though at the same time anarchic tendencies are also on the rise. Hegemonic ambitions are blocking implementation of the 'Agenda for Peace,' which provides for a key peacekeeping role for the UN system. Turbulences on the periphery of world politics are calling forth a 'new interventionism' on the part of world and regional powers.

18. Since the middle of the 1960s there has been a growing number of internal conflicts which, though often referred to as 'ethnic conflicts', are in essence struggles over power and distribution in the guise of 'ethnopolitical' conflicts. The results have included the decay of states, an increase of violence, and uncontrollable disorder in entire regions.

The complexity of today's conflicts rules out any quick-fix solutions imposed from the outside. Solutions proposed by the UN secretaries-general as well as peace research look to a 'primacy of prevention': development of multilateral early-warning systems, quiet mediation diplomacy at several levels, strengthening of the competences of civil society, if need be use of blue helmet troops, control of the arms trade, and development of regional security structures, also with the aid of a development policy conceived as peace policy. One reason why conflict prevention often fails is that the necessary preventive measures, though recognized, are taken not at all, too late, in the wrong sequence, or not consistently. Only in a few exceptional cases has the UN system had the financial and personnel resources it needs for effective prevention.

19. While the end of the East–West conflict meant a worldwide decline in arms spending the peace dividend turned out to be smaller than many had anticipated. The arms trade in and between the OECD countries and the developing countries and countries in transformation is burgeoning. Both the NATO states and some

On the one hand, there has been progress in reducing armament potentials. The US and Russia are negotiating further reductions of their nuclear stockpiles. The UN is undertaking efforts aimed at further developing existing disarmament regimes, outlawing arms exports to crisis regions, and working out a regime for

Eastern European countries continue to be burdened with huge military-industrial complexes. In the South it is China, India, South Africa, and Brazil that are becoming established as arms exporters.

small arms. As in the case of the history of the convention against landmines, NGO lobbying work is playing an important role.

On the other hand, attempts aimed at an effective control of the arms trade have been unable to overcome the interests of the arms exporters. The West is not setting a good example here. The US has refused to sign the landmine convention. The effectiveness of the nuclear non-proliferation treaty is sharply impaired by the refusal of the new nuclear states to join it.

20. The legal institutionalization of human rights and the international protection of human rights is making progress. In this context the project of global governance is becoming the normative foundation of a political world ethics. Acknowledgement of universality and indivisibility of human rights conflicts with the principle of sovereignty, in tendency voiding the principle of non-intervention in the affairs of other states as per Article 2, p. 7, of the UN Charter.

The Vienna Human Rights Conference as well as various UN Human Rights Commission resolutions have recognized the universality and indivisibility of human rights. One other step in the right direction was the institution of the International Criminal Court to prosecute severe violations of human rights. Transnational networks of human rights organizations exercise an important pioneering and corrective function in international human rights policy. Throughout the world their reports continue to document a considerable variety of severe human rights violations, especially in war-torn regions. The recognition in principle of universality and indivisibility has been unable to prevent individual governments from propagating the primacy of 'Islamic values' or 'Asian values', using this cultural relativism as a basis to justify human rights violations; not has this been able to prevent social, economic and cultural human rights from being assigned a back seat, where, under the conditions of mass poverty, they remain far from realization.

Notes on the Contributors

Tanja Brühl, born 1969, Political Scientist, Staff Member at the Department of International Relations at Johann-Wolfgang-Goethe University, Frankfurt. Recent publications include: *Verlust der biologischen Vielfalt: ein neues Problem der internationalen Beziehungen* (AFES Press Report 54), Mosbach 1995; and (with Margareta E. Kulessa), *Patent Protection, Biotechnology and Globalisation: The TRIPs Agreement and its Implications for the Developing Countries*, INEF-Report 31, Duisburg 1998.

Heribert Dieter, born 1961, Economist, Research Fellow at the Institute for Development and Peace (INEF). Recent publications include: *Die Asienkrise: Ursachen, Konsequenzen und die Rolle des Internationalen Waehrungsfonds,* Marburg 1998; and (ed.), *Regionalisation of the World Economy and Consequences for Southern Africa*, Marburg 1997.

Paul Kennedy, born 1945, Professor for International Security Studies at Yale University, New Haven, Connecticut. Recent publications include: *Preparing for the Twenty-First Century*, New York 1993; and *The Rise and Fall of the Great Powers: Economic Change and Military Conflict from 1500 to 2000*, New York 1989.

Dirk Messner, born 1962, Political Scientist and Economist; Executive Director of the Institute for Development and Peace (INEF); Member of the Advisory Commission on Development and Peace of the German Ministry of Foreign Affairs. Recent publications include: *The Network Society. International Competitiveness and Economic Development as Problems of Social Development*, London 1997; *Die Zukunft des Staates*, Bonn 1998; and *Desafíos de la Globalización*, Lima 2000.

Franz Nuscheler, born 1938, Chair of the Department of International Relations at the University of Duisburg; Director of the Institute for Development and Peace (INEF); Member of the German Advisory Council on Global Change of the German Government.

Recent publications include: (ed.), *Entwicklung und Frieden im 21. Jahrhundert. Zur Wirkungsgeschichte des Brandt-Berichts*, Bonn 2000; and (ed. with Dieter Nohlen), *Handbuch der Dritten Welt*, 8 volumes, Bonn, third revised edition 1992–94.

Udo E. Simonis, born 1937, Professor of Environmental Studies at the Social Science Research Center Berlin (WZB); Member of the UN Committee for Development Policy (CDP). Recent publications include: (ed. with Rolf Kreibich), *Global Change – Causal Structures and Indicative Solutions*, Berlin 2000; (ed. with Guenter Altner, Barbara Mettler-von Meibom and Ernst U. von Weizsaecker), *Jahrbuch Oekologie 2001*, Munich 2000.

Index

Compiled by Sue Carlton

Afghanistan 127
Africa
    economic development 69
    and HIV/AIDS 16
    and Internet use 11
Agenda 21 46, 106, 108, 166, 169,
    177
    local 114, 115, 148, 177
Agenda for Peace 167, 179, 180, 192
Annan, Kofi 146, 175, 179
Antarctic Managers Electronic
    Network 49
Arias, Oscar 18
arms trade 16, 18, 129, 193–4
ASEAN (Association of South East
    Asian Nations) 180
Asia crisis 65, 67, 70, 73–6, 141, 171
    and IMF 69, 76, 90, 91
Asia Europe Meeting (ASEM) 80, 81,
    82
Asia-Pacific Economic Cooperation
    (APEC) 80, 81, 82
Association of Small Island States
    (AOSIS) 117

Balkans 16, 127, 137, 138, 141, 150
    see also Kosovo
Bangaladesh 7
banks
    and international law 54–5
    'non-banks' 93
    supervision 93–5, 171
Barber, Benjamin 57
Basel Committee on Banking Super-
    vision 94
Basel Convention on the Control of
    Transboundary Movements of
    Hazardous Waste 121
basic needs pact 169, 174
Bergsten, Fred 86
biodiversity 38, 50, 119, 120

Biodiversity Convention 106, 112,
    113, 116, 117–18
BIS (Bank for International Settle-
    ments) 44, 54, 92, 93, 94, 171
Boutros-Ghali, Boutros 129, 167
Brandt Report 159, 168, 171, 176
Brandt, Willy 157, 159, 165, 176,
    178
Brazil 13, 60, 89
Bretton Woods system, breakdown
    of 24, 82, 172
Brundtland Report 104, 107, 119,
    177
Brzezinski, Zbigniew 134
bubble concept 111–12
Bundesbank 87, 91, 99, 101
Burton, John 24

Cairo World Population Conference
    176, 186
Carlsson, Ingvar 168
Carnegie Endowment for Interna-
    tional Peace 146
'casino capitalism' 147, 153, 166,
    171, 172
Caucasus 127
cement consumption 99
CEPAL 49
Chechnya 150
chemical weapons 14, 16
Chernobyl disaster 24
children, rights of 173, 174
China 60, 67, 133–4, 141, 149, 151
chlorofluorcarbons (CFCs) 108–9
    CFC-free plants 117
civil society 18, 45–6, 168–9, 178,
    181, 193
civilizations, world map of 140
'clash of civilizations' 135, 138–9,
    164
clean-development mechanism
    (CDM) 110, 111, 118

climate 38, 119, 121, 142
  'climate alliance' 115–16
  IPCC (Intergovernmental Panel
    on Climate Change) 49, 110,
    112
  see also gas emissions;
    greenhouse effect; Kyoto
    Protocol
Climate Convention 106, 109, 113,
    118, 190
  enforcement 121
  and NGOs 116
  and US 134
  and voluntary commitments 115
Clinton, Bill 25, 134, 149, 181
CO_2 emissions 99, 112, 115–16
Cold War, end of 80, 125, 126–7,
    130, 165, 167
Cologne Summit 171, 172
Commission on Global Governance
    22, 159, 168
  and cooperative global
    governance 145, 161, 170, 177
  and security 178–9, 180
Commission on Sustainable Devel-
    opment 178
communications 187
  global infrastructure 35, 40–2
Comprehensive Development
    Framework 176
conflict 15, 127, 128, 179–81, 191,
    192–3
  cultural 138–9, 164
  and decolonization 139
  East–West 57, 125, 126, 151, 193
  ethnic 127, 193
  and migration 128, 150, 186
  North–South 129–33
  over resources 56, 128, 192
  prevention 8, 167, 186, 193
  sociopolitical 56
  see also peace/peacekeeping
consumption 99–101
Convention on the Northeast
    Atlantic 121
Convention on the Prevention and
    Punishment of Genocide 150
conventions 112–13, 121, 134, 146,
    150, 194

  see also Biodiversity Convention;
    Climate Convention
cooperation, international 39–40,
    45–6, 144–5, 148–9, 163, 164
Copenhagen World Social Summit
    166, 175, 185, 186
Costa Rica 17–19
Council of Europe 44
CSD, (UN Commission on Sustain-
    able Development) 106–7,
    108, 122, 123
culture
  and conflict 138–9, 164
  and diversity 41, 46, 47–8, 61
  intercultural dialogue 164
  mass 36
  world map of civilizations 140
culture pact 169
currency speculation 77, 88–9, 171
current account balances
  deficits 75–6, 82, 84–5
  surpluses 82, 83–5
Czempiel, Ernst-Otto 26, 88

Dahrendorf, Ralf 33, 142
demilitarization 18, 129
democracy 28, 32, 33, 60, 144, 192
  and human development 17, 19
  universal model 46
democracy pact 169–70
demographic trends 2–7
  regional differences 4–6, 17–19
desertification 128
  see also soil degradation
Desertification Convention 112,
    113, 121
Deutsch Bank 86, 93
Deutschmark/dollar exchange rate
    87
Development and Peace
    Foundation 157
development policy 130–3, 148,
    166–7, 175–6
  and trade policy 174
  transfers to developing countries
    131–2
disease, transborder 16–17
disintegration 32, 127
  'new world disorder' 153, 165, 181

Diversitas 50
Dresdner Bank 86
Dror, Yehezkel 158

earth pact 169
East Asia
  currency speculation 89
  monetary union 87
East Asian Economic Caucus (EAEC) 80, 81
Ebola 16
The Economist 140
ECOSOC (UN Economic and Social Council) 108
ecosystems, destruction of 98
'ecumene concept' 47
Egypt 7
Eisenhower, Dwight D. 6
electricity consumption 100
emissions trading (ET) 110–11
employment and unemployment 18, 188
endangered species 113
energy consumption 13, 38, 100
environment 12–13, 190–1
  causes of degradation 98–102, 176
  'common but differentiated responsibility' 106, 191
  exchange rates 87
  global policy 97–8, 166
    capacity-building 118
    civil society involvement 178
    creating new institutions 122–3
    decision-making procedures 118–20
    financial and technology transfers 117–18
    future options 121–3
    and industrialization 104
    international environmental regimes 108–15, 121–2
    legal enforcement mechanisms 120–1, 122
    national and international levels 102–3, 115
    need for 102–7
    new actors 115–17
    voting rights 118–20

international agreements 113, 120
and multinational corporations 175
and sustainable development 177
world environmental regime 177–8
see also climate; greenhouse effect; ozone layer; pollution
Environmental Protection Agency (EPA) 103
ethnic nationalism 127
euro 66–7, 69, 134–5, 137
euro/dollar exchange rate regime 86–8
European Central Bank 87, 92
European Development Fund 137
European Monetary System 86, 87
European Monetary Union 84
European Union 62, 133, 134, 136–8, 170
  Common Foreign and Security Policy (CFSP) 137–8, 181
  crisis prevention 153
  development policy 137
  protectionism 174
  regional integration projects 30, 43, 69–70
  and US 69, 189
  and world trade order 65
  see also euro
exchange rates 70, 83, 86
  Deutschmark/dollar 87
  euro/dollar 86–8
  stabilization 92, 171
  target zones 86, 87
exploitation, of women and children 173, 176
Extended Structural Adjustment Facility (ESAF) 176

fair trade 174
Falk, Richard 33
FAO (UN Food and Agriculture Organization) 44
fertility rates 3, 5, 7
  see also population
Financial Action Task Force 54–5

financial crises 65, 70, 171, 189
  and foreign investment 131
  and globalization 76–7
  and IMF 69, 76–7, 90–1
  and loans from foreign banks 93
  see also Asia crisis
fish stocks 12, 99, 113
fixed exchange rates 70, 86, 87
flooding 13
foreign debt 132–3, 172–3
  debt relief 172, 176
Forest Declaration 106
forests, clearance of 12, 98
fossil fuels 98
France, current account balance 85
free banking zones 89
free trade
  free trade areas 77, 78–82
  and sustainable development 173
  and welfare gains 174
  and WTO 81, 137, 157
Free Trade Area of the Americas (FTAA) 80
Friends of the Earth 116
fundamentalism 57, 139

G7/G8 135, 165, 171
Galtung, Johan 130, 169
gas emissions 13, 98, 109, 110, 142, 190
  CO_2 99, 112, 115–16
  emissions trading (ET) 110–11
  sinks 98, 112
  see also greenhouse effect
gasoline consumption 100
Gell-Mann, Murray 2
Gender Empowerment Measure(GEM) 177
Gender-related Index (GDI) 177
genocide 150
geo-economics 135
geopolitics 6, 135
Germany
  CO_2 emissions 115–16
  current account balance 85
  customs frontiers 28
  environmental policy 103

Global Environment Facility (GEF) 117, 118, 119
Global Governance 145, 159
global governance 147–9, 158–9
  architecture 38, 44, 59–60, 159–62
  civil society involvement 45–6, 168–9, 178, 181, 193
  and contract theory 168–70
  and cooperation 145–6, 160–1, 163, 170
  and decentralization 147, 160
  international cooperation 39–40, 45–6, 144–5, 148–9, 163, 164
  objections to 149, 181
  and peace 167, 180
  presuppositions of 162–4
  private-public partnership 45, 149, 161–2, 176, 181
  role of United Nations 152, 154, 159, 181
  and superpower governance 149–54
  see also globalization; international law
global market economy *see* world economy
'global risk society' 24, 128–9, 141, 145, 154, 158
global warming *see* greenhouse effect
globalization
  asynchronisms 32–3
  and balance of political power 36
  and conflicting world views 57–8
  and exclusion 32
  and financial crises 76–7
  formation of global structures 30–1
  and fragmentation 32
  and interdependence 141–2, 157, 161
  and labor market 56
  and localization 43, 139, 161
  opportunities and risks 35–6, 157–8
  problem types 38
  process of 29–32
  and regionalization 138, 141, 160, 161

globalization *continued*
  and scientific research 47–50
  significance of 156–9
  unipolar world 134
  and Westernization 57, 139, 157
'glocalization' 139, 161
Goethe, J.W. von 22
grain consumption 99
greenhouse effect 12, 13, 99, 128,
  142, 190
  see also gas emissions
Greenpeace 116
Greenspan, Alan 76
Group of '77 130, 173
Group of Lisbon 147, 158, 168–70,
  174

Habermas, Jürgen 51, 55–6, 146,
  151, 152, 169
HABITAT 106
Haiti 17–19
Hammond, A. 8
hazardous substances 112, 113, 121
Highly Indebted Poor Countries
  (HIPCs) 131–2, 172
HIV/AIDS 16
Hobbes, Thomas 142
Höffe, Otfried 55, 169, 170
human development
  regional differences 17–20
  see also development policy;
  UNDP
Human Development Report 18,
  19, 170, 177
Human Genome Project 49
human rights
  and development 18
  and international law 53–4, 153,
    163–4, 181, 194–5
    see also humanitarian inter-
    vention
  NGOs and 146–7
  UN and 52
  universality of 46, 50, 62, 163,
    164
  and world market 175
  see also poverty
humanitarian intervention 53,
  60–1, 143, 150–2, 181

Huntingdon, Samuel P. 59, 135,
  138–9, 140, 154, 164

ILO (International Labor Organization) 49, 173, 174, 185
IMF (International Monetary Fund)
  44, 89
  assistance loans 92
  and banking supervision 94, 171
  and financial crises 69, 76–7,
    90–1
  policy 74–6
  and poverty reduction 131, 176,
    182
  reform of 90–2
  regionalization of 91–2
  and western interests 174
India 13, 20, 60, 133
individualism 34
Indonesia 67, 73
Industrial Revolution 10
industrialization 101
inflation rates 75
institutional investors 71–4
instrumental activism 34
insurance companies 71–2
integration processes 31
interdependence 23, 26, 32, 38, 136
  concatenated interdependencies
    30–1
  and nation-state 37, 44, 51, 142
interest rates 76, 87
intergovernmental organizations
  (IGOs) 145
international agreements
  enforcement 59
  environment 113, 120
  trade 80
  see also conventions
International Council for Science
  50
International Court of Justice 134
International Criminal Court (ICC)
  45, 56
  and enforcement of international
    agreements 59
  and human rights violations 150,
    153, 163, 181, 194

international financial institutions 123, 135, 165, 182
    see also IMF; World Bank
international financial markets 70–1
    credit relations 92–5
    effect of institutional investors 72–4
    prone to crisis 65, 69, 70, 171
    regulation 65–7, 145, 170, 188–9
    self-regulation 54–5
international financial system
    Keynes Plan 83
    reconstruction of 171–3
    reorganizing monetary regimes 86–8
    Tobin Tax 88–9
    White Plan 83
International Geosphere-Biosphere Program 50
international law 50–6
    and basic needs 174
    enforcement 55–6, 60
    and global unilateralism 59
    and human rights violations 53–4, 153, 163–4, 181, 194–5
    and humanitarian intervention 53, 60–1, 150, 152, 163
    and Internet 54
    and peacekeeping 149, 162
    and state sovereignty 51–3
    and world domestic law 53–6
    and world trade regime 173
international organizations 44–5, 148, 165, 182
    and international law 51, 52
    and scientific research 49–50
    see also NGOs
International Railway Administration 51
international regimes 44–5, 145, 153, 160, 165–6, 181
    environmental 120
    origins of 51
    see also World Trade Organization
International Telegraph Union 51
Internet 24, 29–30, 40, 42
    accessibility 11, 12
    and international law 54

interpenetration, processes of 31
investment, foreign 131
IPCC (Intergovernmental Panel on Climate Change) 49, 110, 112
Iraq 13, 150
Israel 13
Italy, current account balance 85

Japan
    current account surpluses 84–5
    economic crisis 67, 141
    and economic power 133, 134
    foreign aid 131
jihad 57
joint implementation (JI) 110, 111

Kant, Immanuel
    cosmopolitan society 22, 58
    eternal peace 125, 127, 149, 162
    federation of free states 147, 160
    on world state 41
Kazakhstan 69
Kennedy, Paul 134
Kenya 7
Keynes, J.M. 83
Kissinger, Henry 137
Köhler, Claus 86
Kosovo 60–1, 125, 135
    NATO involvement 53, 143, 150–1, 167
Küng, Hans 47–8, 164
Kurds, Iraq 150
Kyoto Protocol 109, 110–12, 121, 190
    flexible mechanisms 110–11, 118

land consumption 99
landmine convention 45, 134, 146, 194
lateral world financial system 43
Latin America, financial crisis 65
Least Developed Countries (LLDCs) 132, 133
Libya 13
localization 43, 139, 161
Lomé Convention 137
Lyme disease 16

'McWorld' 57
malaria 16

marine fish consumption 99
market economy 28, 29, 46
market forces 170–1, 172
Mathews, Jessica 146
MERCOSUR 30, 43
Mexico 136, 171
migration 6–7, 38, 128, 150, 186
military spending 17–18
Le Monde Diplomatique 127
monetary crises 89, 189
monetary regimes, reorganizing
    86–8
money-laundering, international
    54–5
Montreal Protocol 106, 109, 117,
    120
multi-stakeholder dialogue 178
Multilateral Ozone Fund 109, 117,
    119
multilateralism 144–5, 148, 165,
    168, 178, 179–80
    and regionalism 80
    US and 154, 165
multinational corporations 26, 30,
    35, 189
    and international organizations
        45–6
    and NGOs 44
    and social and environmental
        standards 174–5

NAFTA (North American Free Trade
    Agreement) 80
Nairobi, Kenya 105
nation-states 22, 28–9, 36, 37–40,
    61
    and global governance architec-
        ture 59–60, 143–4
    interdependence 37, 44, 51, 142
    and international law 55
    and unilateral decisions 162
    and world society 25, 26, 29, 33,
        36
    see also sovereignty
NATO 137, 138, 182
    involvement in Kosovo 53, 143,
        150–1, 167, 179
    New Strategic Concept 151
    and UN 129, 150, 151, 167, 179

'new development architecture'
    175–6
'new international economic order'
    173
'new international financial archi-
    tecture' 172
'new intransparency' 125, 127, 133
'new weapon states' 13–14, 128,
    192
new world order 125–6, 147
    and 'new world disorder' 153,
        165, 181
Newly Industrialized Countries
    (NICs) 79, 131, 136, 157
NGOs 39, 44, 47, 144, 145–7, 175
    and environmental policy 102,
        116–17, 146, 162, 191
    global players 26, 30
    and international law 50, 54
    and Internet 40, 42
    and landmine convention 194
    transnational networks 146,
        161–2, 170, 182, 187
    at world conferences 45, 116–17,
        146, 162
Nonaligned Movement 126, 129
North Korea 13
nuclear weapons 13–15, 134, 193

OAS (Organization of American
    States) 152, 180
OAU (Organization of African
    Unity) 152, 180
ODA (Overseas Development
    Administration) 131–2
OECD (Organization for Economic
    Cooperation and Develop-
    ment)
    Development Assistance
        Committee (DAC) 180–1, 185
    international research 49
    OECD countries
        current account deficits 85
        and democracy 28
        and development aid 130–1
        and EU 136–7
        and globalization 141, 157,
            158
        and peace 40, 135–6, 153

oil industry 117
organized crime 35, 128
OSCE (Organization for Security
    and Cooperation in Europe)
    44, 137, 138, 151, 152, 180
ozone layer 24, 106, 113, 119, 142
ozone regime 98, 108–9, 120, 190

Pakistan 13
patent applications 10–11
Peace of Westphalia (1648) 28
peace/peacekeeping 52, 125, 134,
    192
    Agenda for Peace 167, 179, 180,
        192
    and development aid 130
    and international law 149, 162
    and OECD countries 40, 135–6,
        153
    world peace regime 178–81
    see also conflict
persistent organic pollutants (POPs)
    112–13
Petrella, Ricardo 168
Philippines 75
PIC Convention (Prior Informed
    Consent) 112
Pinochet Ugarte, Augusto 163
pollution 38, 98, 101, 112–13, 190
POP Regime (persistent organic
    pollutants) 112–13
population development 2–7, 12,
    101–2, 128, 176, 186
    control 7, 166–7, 186
    impact on environment 12,
        101–2
    regional differences 4–6
poverty 1, 7–10, 19, 130, 176, 185
    and population growth 5, 186
    reduction 166–7, 169, 176, 182,
        185
Poverty Reduction and Growth
    Facility 176
protectionism 173, 174

rating agencies 71–4
rationalism 34
Reagan, Ronald 168

regionalism/regionalization 77–82,
    138–41
    and multilateralism 80
    regional cooperation 77, 78
    regional dialogue 77–8, 80–2
    regional integration 31, 77, 78–80
    and world trade order 79–82
religion, and conflict 139
Research Group World Society
    (*Forschungsgruppe Weltge-
    sellschaft*) 26–7
resources
    conflict over 56, 128, 192
    efficient use of 99, 101
    overuse 98, 99, 102
    renewability of 56
Rufin, Jean-Christophe 57–8
Russia
    economic development 68–9,
        127
    financial crisis 65, 90
    nuclear weapons 193
    political power 134, 135, 149,
        150–1

Santayana, George 16
Schlegel, Friedrich von 22
Schmidt, Helmut 76, 92
Scientific Community on Problems
    of the Environment 50
scientific research
    advances in 11
    and ethical problems 35–6, 49
    genetic research 49, 57, 118
    globalization of 47–50
seas
    international waters 119
    law of 106
    oil pollution 113
security 13–15
Senghaas, Dieter 125, 140, 165
Simonis, Udo Ernst 177, 178
Smithsonian Agreement 87
social contracts 24–5
Social Pact 169, 174
socioeconomic disparities 6, 11, 24,
    130, 175, 185
soil degradation 99, 112
    see also desertification

Soros, George 76, 145, 171
South Africa 69
South Korea 67, 73–4, 76, 136
sovereignty 37, 61, 142–3, 148, 165
    and international law 51–3
    shared 161, 180
Soviet Union, collapse of 126–7
Stability Pact for Southeast Europe
    153
Standard & Poor 73
structural adjustment 45, 176
students, studying abroad 49
Subsidiary Body on Technical and
    Technological Advice
    (SBSTTA) 120
Suez Canal 22
sustainable development 106–7,
    148, 173, 177
    Africa 179
    Brundtland Report 104, 177
    Local Agenda 21 114–15, 177
    UN Commission on 106, 108

technological explosion 10–12
    disparities 6, 11–12
    and ethical questions 35–6, 56–7
Teltschik, Horst 76
terrorism, international 128
Thatcher, Margaret 168
'thick morality' and 'thin morality'
    62
Tobin, James 88
Tobin Tax 88–9, 171–2
Töpfer, Klaus 105
Toronto 115
Transatlantic Free Trade Area
    (TAFTA) 80, 81, 82
transnational interaction 30, 43
transportation 190–1
Turkey 16

UNCED, (UN Conference on Envi-
    ronment and Development),
    Rio de Janeiro 104, 106, 107,
    108, 116, 177
UNCTAD (UN Conference on Trade
    and Development) 172
UNDP (UN Development
    Programme) 45, 123, 178, 185

UNEP (UN Environment
    Programme) 104, 105–6, 122,
    123, 128, 178
UNESCO 49, 50, 169
UNFPA (UN Population Fund) 167
unilateralism 59, 162
    United States 134–5, 138, 149,
    165, 179, 181
United Nations
    and arms trade 193–4
    and banking supervision 94–5
    Charter 52, 53, 134, 152, 179,
    192
    Commission on Sustainable
    Development (CSD) 106–7,
    108, 122, 123
    Conference on Environment and
    Development (UNCED), Rio
    de Janeiro 104, 106, 107, 108,
    116, 177
    Conference on Human Environ-
    ment (Stockholm) 97, 103–4,
    107, 116
    Conference on Trade and Devel-
    opment (UNCTAD) 172
    democratization of 169
    Development Programme
    (UNDP) 45, 123, 178, 185
    Human Development Report
    18, 19, 170, 177
    Economic and Social Council
    (ECOSOC) 108
    Environment Programme (UNEP)
    104, 105–6, 122, 123, 128, 178
    environmental policy 103–4
    Food and Agriculture Organiza-
    tion (FAO) 44
    General Assembly 44, 56
    and global unilateralism 59
    Human Rights Commission 169,
    194
    and new world order 125, 129
    and peacekeeping 52, 125, 134,
    179, 180, 192
    Population Fund (UNFPA) 167
    Security Council 52, 149–50, 165
    and global governance 136,
    179

and intervention 129, 134,
    142–3, 151, 152
  and nuclear weapons 13
  reform of 54, 180
United States
  current account deficit 84, 85
  economic cooperation 86–8
  economic growth 67
  and EU 189
  foreign aid 131
  global unilateralism 59
  and landmine convention 194
  and multilateralism 154, 165,
    180
  nuclear weapons 193
  regional integration projects
    69–70
  unilateralism 134–5, 138, 149,
    165, 179, 181
  and world economy 65–7, 81
United States Federal Reserve 87,
    92
Universal Postal Union 22, 51
universalism/universalization 34,
    46–7, 62

Volcker, Paul 86

Walzer, Michael 41, 48
war 8
  see also conflict
Washington Consensus 182
water supplies 12, 13, 99, 128
'water wars' 128
waterfowl habitat 113
weapons of mass destruction 13–15,
    128, 134, 193
welfare state 28, 29, 36
Wells, H.G. 120
West Nile disease 16
Western European Union (WEU)
    137–8
westernization 57, 139, 157
whaling, regulation of 113
White, Harry Dexter 83
WHO (World Health Organization)
    17, 44
women 173, 176–7, 187
wood consumption 99

World Bank 67, 94, 119, 131
  and debt relief 176
  and NGOs 45
  and poverty reduction 19, 182,
    185
  and research programs 49
  and Tobin Tax 172
  and western interests 174
  world economy 187–8
world culture, concepts of 47–8
world economy 24, 42–4, 187–8
  civilizing 36, 46
  growth of 67–70
  and international competitive-
    ness 42–3, 158, 173
  new world economic order 66
  regional collaboration 77–82
  reorganization of 76–7, 171
  stabilizing 82–95
  weaknesses 65–6
World Environment and Develop-
    ment Organization 98, 122–3,
    177–8
World Financial Organization 94–5
World Intellectual Property Organi-
    zation 10
world literature 22
World Monetary Council 83, 85, 92
world politics 58–62, 192–5
  crisis management 135, 164–5,
    167, 172
  turbulence 127, 133
  unipolar or multipolar view
    133–6, 138, 161
  see also new world order
world scientific community 47–8
World Security Council 56
world social regime 174–7
world society 23–7, 184–7
  and global trends 26–7, 127
  and integration 32–3
  new lines of conflict 56–8
  new threats to 128–9
  paradoxes of modernization
    process 34
  political actors of 44–6
  polycentric 35, 147–8
  and social contracts 24–5
  structure of 40, 43–4

world society *continued*
  universal models 46–7, 57
  and world civil rights 163
  'world ethics' 164
  and world politics 58–62
  see also global governance
world state 25, 147, 159–60
  objections to 41
world trade 38, 65
  and debt trap 172–3
  regionalism 79–82

World Trade Organization (WTO)
    65, 95, 123, 145
  and free trade 81, 137, 157
  social and ecological improve-
    ments to 153, 165–6, 173–4
  and western interests 174
world trade regime 173–4, 189
World Wide Fund for Nature
    (WWF) 99, 116

Zollverein (tariff union) 28